Active Questioning
Questioning Still Makes the Difference

by
Nancy L. Johnson

Pieces of
Learning

Cover design by Pat Bleidorn
Layout & Design by Stan Balsamo

©1995 Pieces of Learning

www.piecesoflearning.com

CLC0170
ISBN 1-880505-13-4

Printed in the U.S.A.

TABLE OF CONTENTS

Dedication

Good things come in twos.

To Margaret Manning — who modeled the lifestyle of a professional career woman for her sheltered farm girl niece. Thank you Aunt Marg, for showing me a different way. You were my first hero.

To Kathy Balsamo — my best friend, mentor, business partner, and soul mate. So, who needs a business plan? (Fate had one written from the very beginning!)

Acknowledgements

Stan and Kathy Balsamo for layouts, design, and editing.
Pat Bleidorn for hand lettering and fireworks.
Carolyn Bailey for Spanish questions.
Ken Vinton for pen and ink drawings.

Introduction

"And the beat goes on...and on..." The response to **Questioning Makes The Difference** and **Thinking Is The Key** has been exciting. Teachers, administrators, and parents have voiced their approval in letters, telephone calls, and personal comments at workshops and conferences. And there is a printer in Michigan who will evidence the popularity of both books with several orders for reprints. I am most proud of the multiple orders we have received from college instructors involved in teacher education and school districts using them as a supplemental resource for Staff Development for entire school building staffs. Their enthusiasm and support validate my original contention that differentiated questioning really is the foundation for good teaching and good learning.

However, there is still more work to be done. There is still room for improvement in the area of **student questioning**. It isn't enough for teachers to be good questioners unless their skills are shared with students. The purpose of this book is to provide a wide range of activities and lessons that encourage students to create their own questions not just answer the teacher's questions. It's all just waiting to be applied at the yet to be "teachable moment." Good questions never end, they just multiply...on...and on...and on!

The important thing is not to stop questioning.

A. Einstein

WHO NEEDS THIS BOOK?

Teachers — That's Who!

What questioning does is bring fun and excitement to learning. Differentiated questioning doesn't add to the burdens in the classroom. Most teachers have enough to do. *Questioning — both ACTIVE and PASSIVE — is a teaching tool* to be used at any time, at any grade level, with any curriculum. It is particularly useful for authentic assessment and student portfolios.

Parents and Home Schoolers — That's Who!

Parents *modeling* divergent questioning for their children *strengthens self esteem* and improves school achievement. Many of the life support skills, such as making good decisions, communicating effectively, and solving problems creatively, begin with good questioning.

Curriculum Specialists/Writers and College Instructors — That's Who!

There is an unkind but valid label that is batted around the sacred halls of education. It has to do with what is happening to strong, challenging curriculum. The term is *"dummy down."* Some of the "new" curriculum tries to cover more information without regard for in-depth exploration. Simply put, it's quantity not quality. Differentiated questioning will *stretch the curriculum* so students have time to research and understand ideas.

Special Education Teachers — That's Who!

Whether it is slowing down the learning process or speeding it up, *questioning makes the difference.* Remedial students benefit from questions that simplify while gifted students benefit from those that challenge complexity. Divergent questions allow for differentiated responses from students with special needs.

Kids — That's Who!

Questioning is a learning tool that improves a student's communication abilities and study skills. It does not require a change in learning style or a piece of fancy equipment. All it takes is another human being *modeling* the process and it takes *practice.* Questioning is particularly useful during cooperative learning activities. Students learn to ask as well as answer divergent questions while participating in cooperative groups. This active rather than passive questioning results in a more positive attitude about self and school.

WHY ASK QUESTIONS?
Let's Talk About It

The following ideas might be included in a classroom or family room discussion about the importance of asking questions. Discuss appropriate and inappropriate times and places to ask questions, both at school and at home.

I. Questions are an Important Part of Communication.

Share an experience when a question was answered but you didn't understand. How did that make you feel? What other questions could you have asked to clarify your confusion?

With a partner, role play a conversation with someone who talks and talks and talks but refuses to really answer a question. How does that make you feel?
Can people question with their eyes? their hands? Give examples.

II. Questions Can Help People Avoid Mistakes.

Share an experience at home or at school when you goofed up because you didn't ask enough questions. How did that make you feel?

Discuss the following proverb: "It is better to ask twice than lose your way once."

Who suffers the most when questions are not asked?

How can questions clear up doubts and misconceptions?

What does peer pressure have to do with asking questions?

III. Questions Can Help Improve Study Skills in School.

A student can use self-questioning to organize her thoughts. Before starting a project, a student might ask herself the following questions:

What do I know about this?
What don't I know?
Why am I doing this?
What do I want to accomplish?
What resources will I need?
What if I fail?
What are all the ways I can ask it?
When does it have to be done?
Will I need help?
How do I feel about doing this?

IV. Questions Can Expand Your Thinking and Knowledge.

Discuss times when there is more than one answer to a question. How does it feel to have your own personal point of view?

Share an experience when someone else's question caused you to ask another question.

Share an experience when someone asked you a question that really wasn't a question—it was a command.

What is the difference between a personal and academic question?

Why is a good attitude about questioning important?

Discuss the value of questioning as it relates to jobs and careers.

Discuss the following Rudyard Kipling quote: "Six honest serving men taught me all they knew. Their names are what, why, when, how, where, and who."

THE LANGUAGE OF QUESTIONING

The ACTIVE QUESTIONING process is most effective when teachers start teaching for questions instead of answers. However, when teachers ask students to make up many different questions about a topic, the students not only need a knowledge base about the topic, they also need a knowledge base about questioning. Of the many different kinds of questions, the following five are the most popular and easiest for students to learn and use:

Quantity Questions

Compare/Contrast Questions

Feelings/Opinions/Point of View/ Personification Questions

What if...?

How come...?

I. Quantity Questions

Quantity questions are basically BRAINSTORMING or LISTING questions. However, most teachers ask only REPRODUCTIVE quantity questions. Teachers ask students to reproduce some knowledge or information they already know or should know. Consequently, those kinds of questions slight high level thinking and creativity.

Example: List the parts of a clock.

The other kind of quantity questions is PRODUCTIVE. The students brainstorm as many different ideas as possible—no right/no wrong answers. Teachers should ask both kinds of quantity questions, balancing reproductive and productive thinking.

Example: What are all the ways to tell time other than looking at a clock?

II. Compare/Contrast Questions

Compare/contrast questions (how two things are alike and how they are different) are ideal examples of the development of a simple process into a complex one. They move from the CONCRETE to the ABSTRACT. The following examples compare and contrast two objects, ideas, or concepts from the same category. Gradually progress to more difficult/complex categories that require forced associations.

Example: Ask students to choose partners. Have them hold out and examine their left hands. Ask partners to compare/contrast hands. Share responses with their partners. Ask students to compare/contrast their hands to cooking tongs. Ask students to compare/contrast cooking tongs and a can opener.

Forced Association: How are computers and can openers alike/different?

III. Feelings/Opinions/Point of View/Personification Questions

Feelings/opinions/point of view/personification questions are a powerful, exciting teacher tool. They are fun and challenging for teachers to model as well as teach. These questions pull teacher and student together on an emotional level.

Example: (Feelings) Which season of the year makes you feel happy? Which makes you feel tired? Which makes you feel lazy? Why?

Example: (Opinion/Point Of View) In your opinion, should state government pass a law forcing bicycle riders to wear helmets?

Example: (Personification) How would a flagpole feel about a 1000 pound flag?

There is an interesting "fringe benefit" with these questions. They open the door to MOTIVATION. The hidden force that motivates is EMOTION. These questions are charged with emotion, especially when they fit the student's age, interests, and abilities.

IV. What if...? or What would happen if...? Questions

Kids will say these questions are just plain fun. To completely let go of rigid thinking patterns, to break traditional mind sets, to open the mind to an "anything goes" attitude has to be one of life's greatest highs. The teacher who facilitates "What would happen if?" questions must accept the responsibility as leader and model for laughter, creative thinking, and active questioning. "SERIOSITY" is a block to the whole process. Laughter is the key that unlocks divergence. Students need to see and analyze adults using the divergent questioning process. They also need guidance in moving from divergent thinking to convergent thinking.

Example: What if human beings did not have tongues?

V. How come...? Questions

Questions that begin with "How come..." require higher level thinking skills than questions that begin with "How...". They are the best example of the philosophy that questions are more important than answers. How come...? questions are not meant to be answered. The fun and creativity is in how many you can come up with, not whether or not there is a logical answer.

Example: How come jumbo shrimp are so small?

Questioning: ACTIVE vs. PASSIVE

It's true. We teach kids to answer. We don't teach them to question. Actually we condition kids to answer. Playing the school game means learning how to come up with the right answer. In a very short time kids learn how to "do good school." They should be learning how to "do good life." Asking questions, not just answering them, is a life support skill, maybe even a survival skill. It is connected to decision making and problem solving.

There is more thinking and learning in asking questions than in answering them. The question is more important than the answer. Once a question is answered, the inquiry process STOPS! However, who asks most of the questions in most classrooms? The answer: The teacher! According to J.T. Dillon, teachers ask 80 questions per hour compared to only 2 questions per hour from all the students combined.

OK. Let's think this through — logically. If teachers are asking most of the questions and there is more thinking and learning in questioning, then who is doing most of the thinking and learning in most classrooms? Once again, the answer is teachers. OOPS! Isn't there something wrong with this picture?

It's time to change that picture. It's time to turn classrooms into think tanks overflowing with inquiry. It's time to teach kids how to ask questions, not just answer them. The good news is, it's easy! Just remember two words, ACTIVE and PASSIVE. When kids answer questions it is a passive process. When they ask questions it becomes an active process.

Start with homework. Instead of giving students a page of math problems to solve, give them one answer and ask them to make up as many different math problems as they can that have that answer. The key words here are "many" and "different." When students solve a page of math problems they must do or use mathematics. Most of the time that is a lower level thinking process. When they make up or create their own math problems they must think mathematically. That is a higher level thinking process.

PASSIVE Questions

Are Those <u>Answered</u> By The Student

ACTIVE Questions

Are Those <u>Asked</u> By The Student

Objectives For
Active Questioning

1. The student will demonstrate an ability to articulate questions clearly during partnering and/or group activities.

2. The student will use convergent and divergent active questioning to undertake library research in order to gather data for the completion of assignments.

3. The student will use active questioning skills to apply, analyze, synthesize and evaluate printed materials to accomplish learning activities.

4. The student will use mindMaps to demonstrate an understanding of the five types of active questioning: **Quantity, What if...?, Point of View, Compare/Contrast, and How come...?.**

5. The student will use active questioning to develop a more positive self concept by recognizing and using his/her abilities, becoming more self-directed and appreciating likenesses and differences among himself/herself and others.

6. The student will use active questioning to produce examples of authentic assessment for a personal portfolio.

7. The student will show originality by expressing unusual, uncommon responses while composing questions.

8. The student will use active questioning techniques to describe his/her feelings and values.

9. The student will predict many different causes/effects for given situations by creating many varied divergent questions.

10. The student will use active questioning skills to recognize the goals and objectives of a group by working toward consensus in cooperative learning situations.

TEACHER EVALUATION

Questions for Administrators and Supervisors:

Question # 1: Are Your Teachers Good Questioners?

Question # 2: How Can You Tell?

Question # 3: How Can You Improve Their Questioning Skills?

Hopefully we have reached a point in education where administrators/supervisors serve as instructional leaders as well as jugglers of schedules and budgets. Effective, restructured schools house principals and supervisors who spend much of their time in classrooms observing teachers and making recommendations.

Practice What You Preach

There is no doubt about it. We ALL must model what we teach. Administrators and supervisors are teachers too. They cannot expect teachers to use good questioning techniques unless they model the same themselves. Classroom demonstrations, staff meetings, conferences with parents, conversations with students, recommendations to support staff, school board meetings, and presentations at conventions are all opportunities where administrators/supervisors can take advantage of a questioning "teachable moment."

A non threatening, positive method of encouraging teachers to work on those questioning techniques which need improvement is to:

• Share ideas from resource materials that exemplify the divergent thinking/ questioning philosophy.

• Model those ideas during classroom demonstrations. (If the administrator/ supervisor is not qualified or able to demonstrate the skills, then the teacher should be allowed to leave the classroom and observe a peer who is successful in using divergent questioning strategies.)

• Use the TEACHER CHECKLIST on pages 18 & 19 to evaluate the teacher and determine how many of the ideas are being applied. Several days or weeks may separate each step to allow teachers adequate time to prepare and practice the strategies.

A copy of the checklist should be given to the teacher well in advance of the evaluator's visit so that the teacher can use it for self evaluation. When the checklist is used as part of the formal teacher evaluation process, it becomes a useful discussion guide and planning tool for change and improvement.

THE BEST ADVICE

There are two recommendations that administrators/supervisors can offer teachers which they can begin practicing immediately without any preparation.

1. Slow down! Give students more time to respond. Dr. Madeline Hunter's research indicated that a typical teacher waits only 2.5 seconds for a student to respond to a question. Encourage teachers to slowly work up to a "wait time" of 10 seconds or more.

2. Stop answering ALL your own questions! Again, Dr. Hunter's research indicates teachers answer nearly 90% of their own questions. Encourage teachers to slowly lower that percentage to 50% or less.

Questioning Makes The Difference
Teacher Checklist

Teacher's Name_____   Grade/Class/Subject_____
Date of Taping or Observation___/___/____   Length of Taping or Observation____
Name of Observer (if other than teacher)_____

Low Level Thinking ⟶ High Level Thinking

Graph To Plot Total Number of Questions

50
45
40
35
30
25
20
15
10
5
0

Tally for Questions ⟶

Type of Questions	Recall Right/Wrong Answer	Rep. Quantity	Pro.	Compare Contrast Forced Assoc.*	Feelings Opinions Person.	What If?	Active Ques.	Passive Ques.
Examples of Questions	What is 2 + 2? Who was America's 13th first lady? When did man walk on the moon?	Reproductive: List the kinds of doors and windows in the room.	Productive: List all the ways to get out of the room.	How is ____ like ____? How is ____ different from ____? * Forced Association: Compare/ Contrast spiders and cars.	Would you rather eat pizza or watermelon? WHY? Personification: How would a bear feel about a bear trap?	What would happen if humans did not have thumbs?	Student generated: Compose a list of questions a zoo might ask a tiger in the wild.	Teacher or textbook generated: All forms of questions qualify.

18

To The Teacher:

Reflections of My Personal Questioning Style

Readiness

From a Good Resource
THINKING IS THE KEY
© 1992
Pieces of Learning

Reflect and comment on the following:

Did I take a moment to think about the physical environment, atmosphere, and tone of my classroom? _____

What things did I do to change any of the above?_____

_____

How did I influence the attitudes of my students toward learning before the lesson was taught? _____

_____

What questions did I use to focus and center students' thinking before the lesson was taught? _____

_____

The Questioning Process

Reflect and comment on the following:

Did I wait at least 8 to 10 seconds for students to answer my questions?_____

Did I answer most of my own questions?_____

Which kind of question did I ask most? _____
Least?_____

About what percent of my questions were passive?_____active?_____

Did I call on more boys than girls?_____girls than boys?_____

Follow-up Improvement Plan

I need to ask more of these kinds of questions: _____
I repeat this checklist and reflection page on _____. I expect the following to have
                                              (date)
improved:

Students should feel proud that they have a question rather than pleased that they have the answer.

Janice Szabos

Active questioning takes students out of the passive or response mode and encourages them to set their own agenda for exploration. Student questions take center stage, and the formulation of all kinds of questions about any topic being addressed is not only accepted, but also expected.

Janice Szabos
Former Director
Gifted Education
Fairfax County, VA

APPLICATION

The teaching/learning process breaks down if the teacher and learner do not apply the questioning techniques. Just as learning about riding a bicycle is not the same as actually riding one, learning about questioning and actually learning questioning are two very different things. The difference is application.

A near-synonym for application is practice. We just can't sugar-coat the process and expect good questioning to happen in one or two easy lessons. First, teachers must make a commitment to include differentiated questioning in their own thinking. Then, personal application is the best practice. Teachers will gain the confidence they need to use the skills in the classroom by using divergent questions to solve personal and work-related problems.

Another near-synonym for application is infusion. Differentiated questioning should never be taught in isolation. It is a way of thinking, a philosophy.

A few months ago, while fulfilling a consulting contract in a local school district, I asked the building administrator if her teachers were doing anything to improve questioning skills. She replied, "Oh yes! We do that in the spring. We have a grant that is two weeks long. We do questioning in April!" Making divergent questions part of every class, every subject, every day is what infusion really means.

The activities and lessons in this book will give students the opportunity they need to apply their ACTIVE QUESTIONING skills in creative thought provoking ways. Remember! With just a little practice students get really good at this "stuff".

Low Level Thinking or High Level Thinking
So Which is It?

It is important that teachers and parents model different kinds of questions that stimulate higher level thinking. The list below is based on "Little Red Riding Hood," but the concept can be applied to all levels of literature.

"The Adventures of Little Red"

Low Level Thinking

> How many little girls are there in the story?
> What happened first in the story?
> Where was Little Red going?
> What color was Little Red's cape?
> What did the wolf do to trick Little Red?
> Who was the senior citizen living in the house?
> Was Little Red walking alone in the woods?
> Did Little Red know where she was going?
> Was Little Red a child or a teenager?
> How did the story end?

High Level Thinking

> Would you rather be the wolf or Little Red? Why?
> Are real wolves like the one in the story?
> Do you know any other stories about wolves?
> What are all the ways Grandma could have protected herself?
> Do you think most grandmas look forward to visits from their children?
> What is your opinion about the intelligence of this wolf?
> What other endings to the story might be possible?
> What is the difference between fact and fiction?
> Compare/contrast the wolf and Grandma.

_____

(Title of story or book)

Low Level Thinking Questions

1. Who_____?

2. What_____?

3. Where_____?

4. When_____?

5. How_____?

6. Why_____?

7. _____?

High Level Thinking Questions

1. What are all the ways_____?

2. What if_____?

3. How is _____ different from_____?

4. What is your point of view about_____?

5. How come_____?

6. How do you feel about_____?

7. _____?

Applying Bloom's Taxonomy
To "The Adventures of Little Red"

Knowledge:

Who is the main character?
Where was Little Red going?
List words in the story that are new to you.

Comprehension:

Draw two scenes from the story.
Why was Little Red going to Grandma's house?
Write a paragraph using five of the new words from the story.

Application:

Write a telephone conversation between Little Red and her grandmother.
Describe a place that you have visited that is like the setting of this story.
Write a letter to the wolf from Little Red.

Analysis:

What parts of the story could not have actually happened?
Pick one character from the story and write five questions from his/her point of view.
Compare/contrast your own grandmother's house with the grandmother's house in the story.

Synthesis:

How might the story have been different if Little Red had visited your own house?
What if the wolf owned a travel agency? Design a travel brochure for the places in the story from the wolf's point of view.
What if you added another character to the story? Write a new ending from the new character's point of view.

Evaluation:

What if you were the wolf in the story? Defend your actions and feelings in the story.
Would you rather live where the story takes place or where you live now? Why?
Do you think Little Red was happy before she met the wolf? What about after?

Applying Bloom's Taxonomy

(Title of story or book)

Knowledge:
Who is the main character?
Where was _____ going?
List words in the story that are new to you.

Comprehension:
Draw two scenes from the story.
Why was _____?
Write a paragraph using five of the new words from the story.

Application:
Write a telephone conversation between _____ and _____.
Describe a place that you have visited that is like the setting of this story.
Write a letter to _____from _____.

Analysis:
What parts of the story could not have actually happened?
Pick one character from the story and write five questions from his/her point of view.
Compare/contrast_____ with _____.

Synthesis:
How might the story have been different if_____?
What if _____?
What if you added another character to the story? Write a new ending from the new character's point of view.

Evaluation:
What if you were the _____ in the story? Defend your actions and feelings in the story.
Would you rather live where the story takes place or where you live now? Why?
Do you think _____? Why?

Everything But the Kitchen Sink!

In partners or groups brainstorm items which you think the Pilgrims might have taken with them on their voyage to the new world. Prioritize 5 items on your list. Compare/contrast your list with other groups.

Mayflower Cargo Manifest

_____

_____

_____

_____

_____

_____

_____

_____

_____

_____

_____

Five Most Important Items

1._____

2._____

3._____

4._____

5._____

Make a list of all the things the Pilgrims wished they could have taken with them to the New World.

_____

_____

_____

_____

_____

_____

_____

_____

Make a list of all the things the Pilgrims DIDN'T take with them on the Mayflower. Why not?

_____

_____

_____

_____

_____

_____

_____

_____

ACTIVE Questioning

Compose a list of questions that the Pilgrims might have asked Mayflower Captain Christopher Jones before the start of their journey.

_____

_____

_____

_____

_____

_____

_____

More ACTIVE Questioning

Combine Quantity questions and What if...? questions. Example:
What might have been on the cargo list of the Mayflower if.....
. . . the year had been 1912? 2012? or 512?
. . . the Mayflower had been a hot air balloon?
. . . the royal family had been along?
. . . the destination had been _____?

Now make up your own Quantity/What if questions:

_____

_____

_____

_____

Everything But the Kitchen Sink!

The Real Thing

The actual cargo that the Pilgrims and other passengers brought with them when they traveled on the Mayflower to the New World included the following:

Food

oats	hogsheads of rye	ship's biscuits	lemons for scurvy
dried beans	wheat	dried peas	barrels of olive oil
turnips	casks of beer	wine	firkins of butter
barley	water	salted beef	seeds for planting
salted fish	salt	pickled eggs	gammons of bacon
pickled cowcumbers (cucumbers)			

Guns and Armor

helmets	swords	breast and back plates	cutlasses
pikes	halberts	muskets	

Household Furnishings

candlesticks	linens	clothes	trenchers (plates)
chairs	bedsteads	bedding	needles and thread
tables	buckets	rush lamps	mortars and pestles
cradles	spinning wheels and looms		
butter churns	cooking utensils and dishes		
chests packed with ruggings (blankets)			

Tools

hoes	rakes	plow heads	spades
hooks	lines	axes and saws for felling trees	
nets for fishing	tools for forging nails, building houses and furniture, and repairing shoes		

Books (Books were among the most prized possessions of the Pilgrims.)

religious books, including the Bible, psalters for psalm singing
almanacs   some writing of Aristotle   medical books brought by the surgeon

Animals

hens   roosters   two dogs

Everything But the Kitchen Sink!

Creative Writing

Directions: Write a journal entry using this introduction.

The weather was stormy. After our lunch of dried beans and pickled eggs we went below to take a look into the only trunk Mother was allowed to bring. Inside we found...

_____

_____

_____

_____

_____

_____

_____

_____

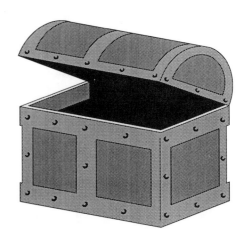

Draw your ideas.

"Pen" Pal Pets

Do you have a "pen pal?" Not a friend that you write to, but a pet that lives in a pen? A pet mouse? A gerbil? A snake? What do you have? What would you like to have?

What's good about life "in the pen."	What's bad about life "in the pen."
_____	_____
_____	_____
_____	_____
_____	_____
_____	_____
_____	_____

What's good about having an owner? (From the pet's point of view)

_____

_____

_____

_____

_____

From a Good Resource
IMAGI-SIZE
by Rita Milios
Pieces of Learning
© 1993

Eye On Japan

A friend and fellow author, Carolyn Coil visited Japan in 1990. Fortunately she kept a journal during her travels to this fascinating country. In 1994 the journal was transformed into a delightful activity book that is a wonderful resource for comparing and contrasting our American culture with that of the Japanese. Her observations of schools and everyday life in Japan are the basis for the following questioning activities.

...there were no custodians and the students cleaned your school?
...you rode a motorbike to school?

...your school band only had girls in it?
...your grade in each subject was based on two exams per year?

...almost all of the teachers in your school were men?
...everyone had to wear a uniform to school?

What If...?

...all high school students had to wear uniforms?
...coaches did not receive exta pay for after school sports?

...no high school students were allowed to drive?
...there was no substitute when your teacher was absent?

...all students went to school 1/2 day on Saturdays?

CHALLENGE
Find out the size of Japan and the number of people who live there. Find out the same information about the United States. Then list ten differences in the two countries that may be caused by the differences in the amount of space available to people in each country.

Eye On _____
(name of country)

_____

_____

(fact about the country)

_____

_____

_____

_____

What If...?

_____

_____

_____

_____

_____

_____

_____

_____

Challenge:

_____

_____

_____

Questioning on the Move: "PREFERENCE"

Have you heard? The brain is hooked to the body! More brain cells are stimulated when the human body is thinking on its feet. Remember some of those "old fashioned" teaching techniques: standing up to read, standing up to ask questions, standing up to answer. Maybe it's time to make *standing up* fashionable again.

Ask students to stand in a group in front of the teacher. The teacher begins the activity with the following instructions:

"This activity is called **PREFERENCE**. *Try to imagine that I am standing on a dividing line down the middle of the room. In just a moment I will ask all of you a question. You will show your answers by moving to either side of the dividing line. For example, if you could live in only one season of the year and your choices were winter (teacher points to left side of room) or summer (teacher points to right side of the room) which would you choose? Move to the side of the room that you prefer. Don't stand on the line. You may like both seasons or you may hate both. (Maybe spring is your favorite!) Try to choose anyway."*

After students have moved to the side they prefer, the teacher asks for oral responses. *"You have shown your opinion by moving to one side of the room. Can you support your opinion by sharing your reasons with the class?"* Do not expect all students to respond verbally. It is important to establish a fairly high comfort level, so don't put students on the spot by forcing them to answer. This activity not only gets kids up off their backsides, it gives even the shyest student the chance to participate by *"showing"* opinions instead of voicing them.

Note: It is important that the teacher NOT give students permission to stand on the line. However, in some instances a student may either have very strong feelings about both or no feelings about either choice. Use this as a "teachable moment." Choosing not to choose is, in fact, a choice. This is the time a student must give strong, valid reasons for not choosing.

An alternative: Put strips of tape on the floor, left to right, an equal distance apart. One end is designated *"stongly agree"* and the other is designated *"strongly disagree."* Students stand on the point of the continum where they are comfortable relative to the ends. Continue the activity by asking the following questions:

"If you could be awake only half the day, would you prefer DAYTIME or NIGHTIME? Would you rather wear SHOES or BOOTS? Which tastes better HAMBURGERS or CHICKEN SANDWICHES? Which would you rather do — HEAR A CD or GO TO A CONCERT? Which is more fun to do — MATH or SPELLING? Which would you rather do — USE A COMPUTER or HAND WRITE A REPORT?"

In the following list, several of the choices are high risk and deserve time and discussion. Ask students to do their own preference list as homework.

"PREFERENCE" Questions

Would you rather be
the wind or a river

Would you rather be
a pillow or a blanket

Would you rather
be a quarterback or receiver

Which would you rather have
spiked hair or pierced ears

Would you rather be
a postcard or a FAX

If you played both well,
which would you choose
basketball or baseball

Would you rather be
a snowflake or a raindrop

Would you rather be
**a computer programmer
or a nurse**

Would you rather be
**a Venus fly trap or
a butterfly net**

Would you rather be
a breakfast or a dinner

Would you rather be
a milkweed plant or a rose

Would you rather be
**an ice cream cone or
a banana split**

Would you rather be
**President of the United States
or a rock star**

Would you rather be
a snow shovel or a lawn mower

Would you rather be
**a Fisher-Price™ toy or
a Monopoly™ game**

Would you rather be
a big red barn or a skyscraper

Where would you most like
to spend your spare time
in the Mall or at an art gallery

If you had to lose one,
which would you choose
**the ability to speak or
the ability to walk**

Would you rather be
a hic-up or a burp

Would you rather be
a leaf or a rock

Should a helmet law
be required in all 50 states
yes or no

Would you rather live
**near the ocean or
in the mountains**

Is it better to get the news by
**watching television or
reading the newspaper**

Should school in the United States
be year round
yes or no

Would you rather be
spring or fall

Would you rather be
**a giant oak tree
or a tiny hummingbird**

Suppose you were on the jury
and you believed the crime
justified it. Would you vote for
death penalty or life in prison

As an occupation,
would you rather be
**a painter of suspension bridges
or an engineer on a submarine**

Would you rather be
**a potato chip or
a piece of candy**

Would you rather be
**an apartment building
or a racetrack**

Do you think it is a good idea
to announce warnings
before TV shows broadcast
shows that contain violence
yes or no

Would you eat a bowl of live worms
for $50,000
yes or no

More questions suggested by teacher:

Student "PREFERENCE" Questions

To the student: Develop a list of "Preference" questions that you would like to ask your classmates.

_____

_____

_____

_____

_____

_____

_____

_____

_____

Dealing with Student Responses

Don't forget timing and comfort level. Students will respond more honestly if they trust the facilitator of the activity. Start with low risk choices such as the season of the year, foods, television shows, etc. Expect students to change their minds and switch sides during the activity. Discuss their reasons for doing so. (After all, don't we adults sometimes change horses in the middle of the stream?) Combining opinions and changing your mind is a true form of synthesis.

LISTEN to their opinions. Expect strong emotions to surface as the high risk questions are asked. Be prepared to take time to help students analyze their choices and their feelings.

"Did you choose one side because you didn't like the other side?"
"Did you dislike both choices and the one was the lesser of two evils?"
"Did you wait for your best friend to choose and then you followed his/her lead?"
"How does it feel to be part of the majority/minority side?"
"Is it ok to have a different preference/opinion?"

The word is acceptance. The concept is agreeing to disagree.

The teacher/facilitator must be careful not to "beat a dead horse" and over analyze each and every student response. Timing is important. Keep the activity moving.

In responding to unusual or divergent opinions, use the response, *"That's good thinking!"* When the response is *"That's a good answer,"* the implication is it must be the right answer. And a right answer means there must be a wrong answer. That is NOT what this activity is about. There are no right or wrong answers in this activity, just answers — opinions and feelings. One final suggestion: the teacher/facilitator should withhold his/her personal opinions.

Personification Questions

What fun! To be able to speak for someone or something else—to see things from a DIFFERENT POINT OF VIEW.

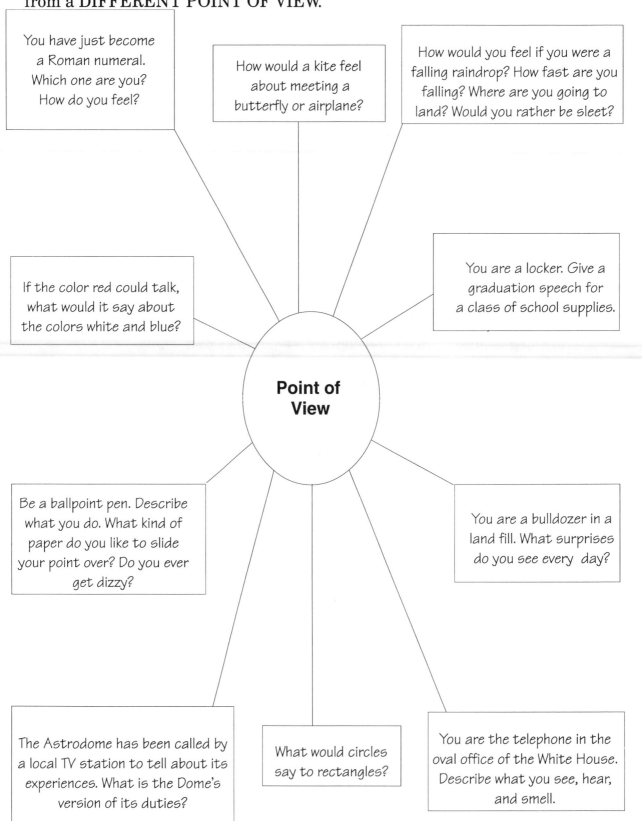

You have just become a Roman numeral. Which one are you? How do you feel?

How would a kite feel about meeting a butterfly or airplane?

How would you feel if you were a falling raindrop? How fast are you falling? Where are you going to land? Would you rather be sleet?

If the color red could talk, what would it say about the colors white and blue?

You are a locker. Give a graduation speech for a class of school supplies.

Point of View

Be a ballpoint pen. Describe what you do. What kind of paper do you like to slide your point over? Do you ever get dizzy?

You are a bulldozer in a land fill. What surprises do you see every day?

The Astrodome has been called by a local TV station to tell about its experiences. What is the Dome's version of its duties?

What would circles say to rectangles?

You are the telephone in the oval office of the White House. Describe what you see, hear, and smell.

Personification Questions

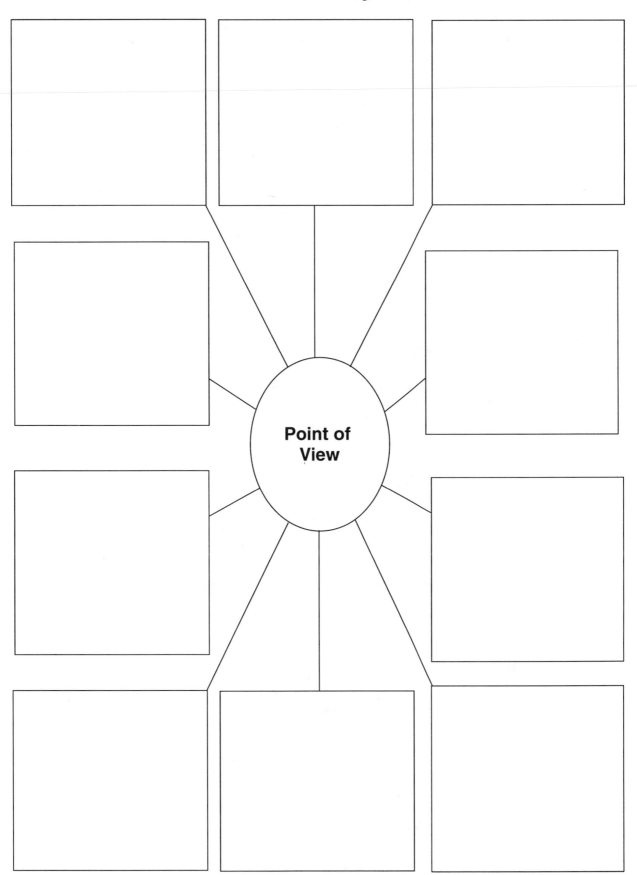

Mindbranching

For every action there is a reaction. Use the following questions to motivate your mind to "branch out" in a different direction. How many MORE mind-branching questions can you think of ?

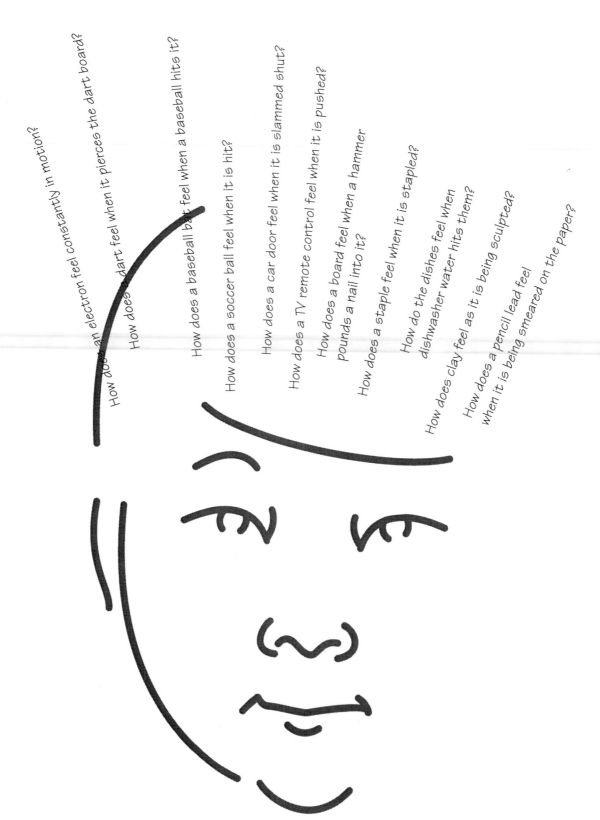

How does an electron feel constantly in motion?

How does a dart feel when it pierces the dart board?

How does a baseball bat feel when a baseball hits it?

How does a soccer ball feel when it is hit?

How does a car door feel when it is slammed shut?

How does a TV remote control feel when it is pushed?

How does a board feel when a hammer pounds a nail into it?

How does a staple feel when it is stapled?

How do the dishes feel when dishwasher water hits them?

How does clay feel as it is being sculpted?

How does a pencil lead feel when it is being smeared on the paper?

Mindbranching

Now it's your turn! List as many different Mindbranching questions as you can.

A Learning Log Using Questions

I WONDER....?

_____'s Question Journal
name of student

How many QUESTIONS did I ask today? (circle one)

1-3   3-6   6-9   10 or more

What was the most_____QUESTION I heard today?

important   crazy   beautiful   scary   strange
sad   difficult   funny   frustrating

What QUESTION did I ask that didn't get answered today?_____

_____

What QUESTION should I have asked, but didn't?_____

_____

I was just wondering_____

_____

How come_____

_____

What if_____

_____

What QUESTION really made me angry today?_____

_____

What QUESTION do I need to think more about before I respond?_____

_____

With no help from Socrates, children everywhere are schooled to become masters at answering questions and to remain novices at asking them. The normal practice is to induce in the young answers given by others to questions put by others. A complementary practice would induce STUDENT QUESTIONS, forming their answers in the public light of joint inquiry.

J.T. Dillon

A Grab Bag of Questions
WHAT IF...?

What if all the clothes in the world were made of paper?

What if you became a host on MTV?

What if people couldn't talk—only musical notes came out?

What if you found out the new President of the United States was your aunt?

What if a giant meteor was scheduled to hit the earth in two weeks?

What if there were no boxes in the world?

What if a cheap new fuel for cars was found in only one small country in Africa?

What if you had to move to a different town every year?

What if you were sentenced to life in prison without parole?

What if people ate only one meal a day?

What if you could examine the personal possessions of a famous person? Who would you choose?

What if you could trade places with one of your parents?

What if everyone in the world had a buddy?

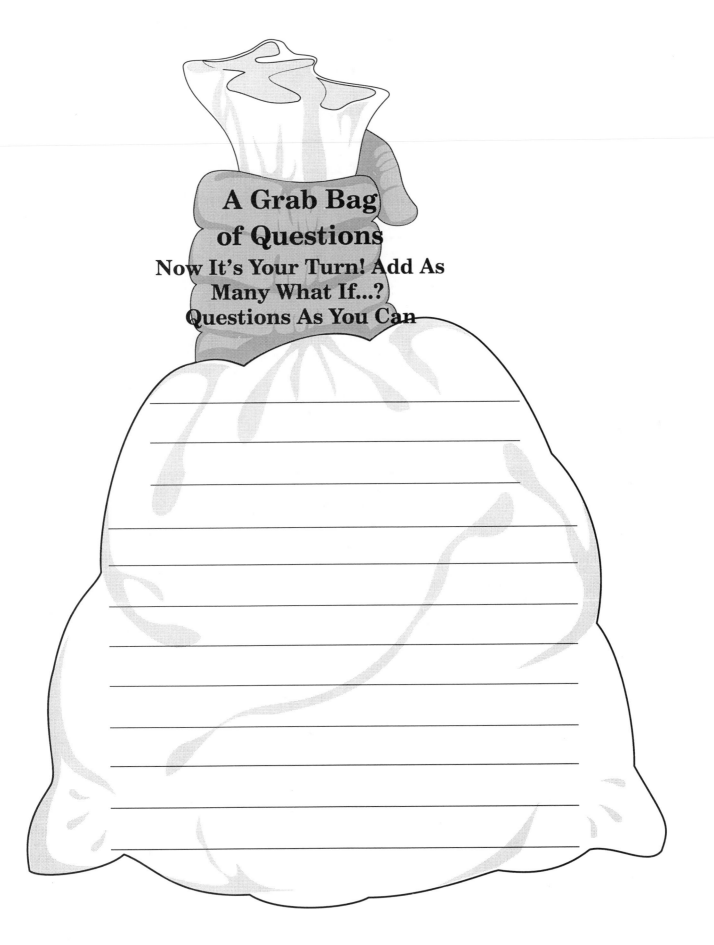

A Grab Bag of Questions

Now It's Your Turn! Add As Many What If...? Questions As You Can

A Wheel of Questions

Compose a question that:

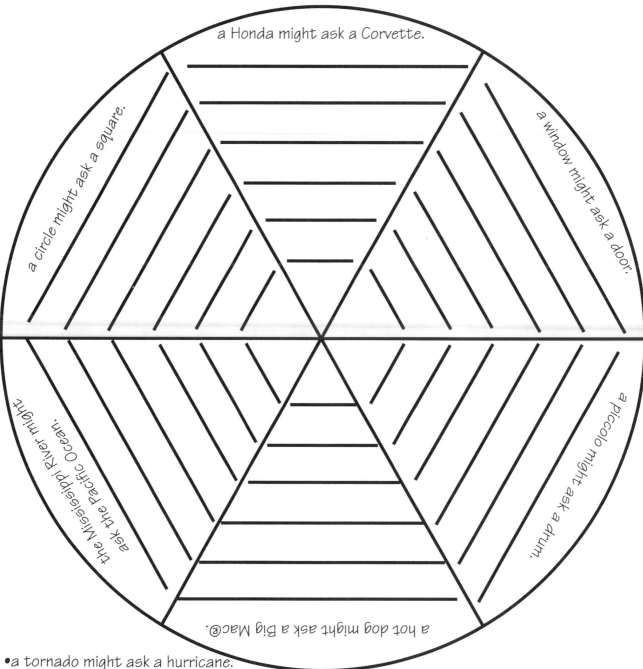

a Honda might ask a Corvette.

a window might ask a door.

a circle might ask a square.

the Mississippi River might ask the Pacific Ocean.

a piccolo might ask a drum.

a hot dog might ask a Big Mac®.

• a tornado might ask a hurricane.
• Louis and Clark might ask Neal Armstrong.
• a golf club might ask a tennis racket.
• a Valentine's Day card might ask a Halloween Card.

• Thomas Jefferson's quill pen might ask Norman Rockwell's paint brush.

• the President of the United States might ask the CEO of General Motors.

Spinning Questions

Spin the arrow and
make up questions
about:
toys
popcorn
sharks

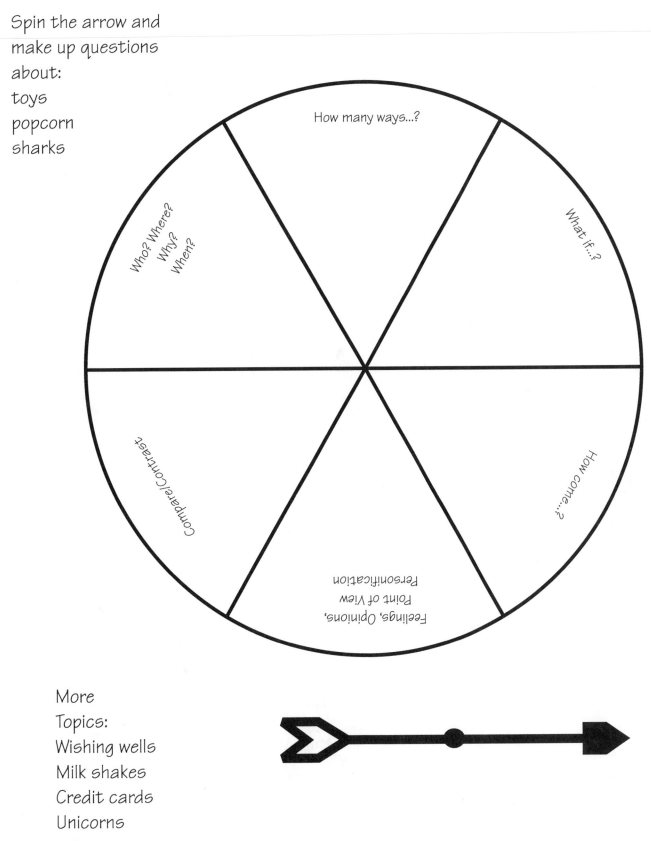

More
Topics:
Wishing wells
Milk shakes
Credit cards
Unicorns

Spinning Questions

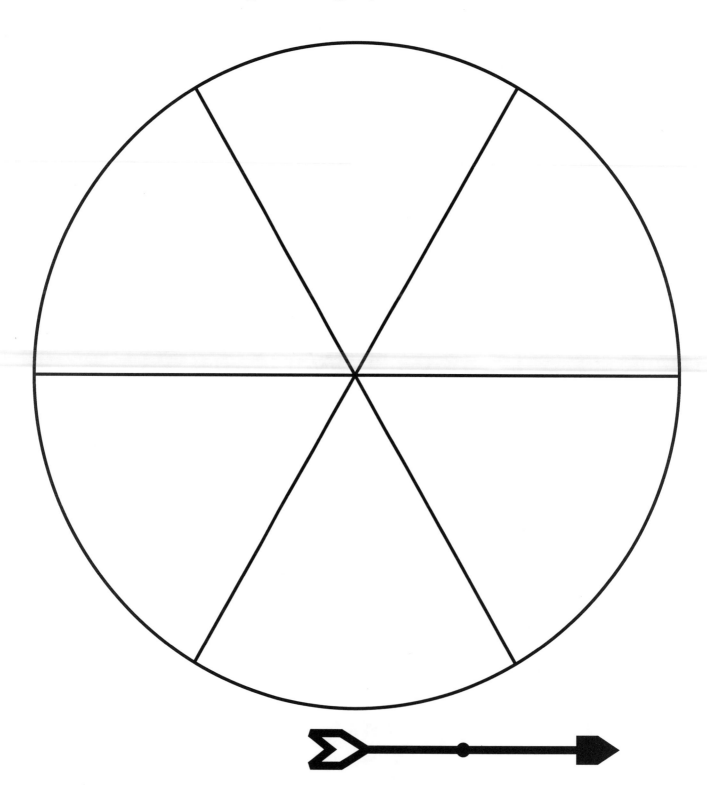

When students do not ask questions, both teaching and learning suffer. J.T. Dillon

Circles of Yarn

Remember the brain really is hooked to the backside! Involve students in a compare/contrast READINESS activity before they begin composing compare/contrast questions. The very best readiness activities combine INTELLECT, EMOTION, and BODY. A simple piece of yarn and a little teacher directed instruction will stimulate all three.

Arrange students in groups of four or five in a large, open space such as a learning center, gym, or playground. Give each group a piece of yarn 10 to 12 feet long that has the ends tied together in a closed circle. The teacher directed instruction involves math, language arts, and social studies. Students may respond to each part of the activity verbally or nonverbally depending on the teacher's instructions.

Each compare/contrast yarn activity begins with each group of four or five students standing in a circle holding on to a part of the *"Circle of Yarn."*

MATH

Teacher: *"Using your circle of yarn and the people in your group, show me MORE THAN inside the circle and LESS THAN outside."* (More students in each group move to the inside of their yarn circle while less remain on the outside of the yarn circle.)

"Show me an empty circle." (All students move to the outside of the yarn circle.)

"Show me LESS THAN inside the circle and MORE THAN outside the circle." (More students in each group move to the outside of their yarn circle while less remain on the inside of the yarn circle.)

"Show me an empty circle."

"Show me more than two but less than five inside your circle of yarn." (Three or four students in each group move to the inside of the circle.)

"Show me an empty circle."

"Using the correct number of people inside the circle, show me the answer to the following problem: 2+2+1-2 X 1=?"

"Show me an empty circle."

"With each group member holding on to parts of the circle of yarn, make the following shapes. Remember! Everybody hold on to the yarn. Make a circle, square, triangle, rectangle, equilateral triangle, pentagon, standing right triangle, isosceles triangle, hexagon." (Give the groups a couple of minutes to make each shape. Teacher walks among the groups to check the responses.)

"Can you make two triangles with your circle of yarn?"

"Can you make four triangles with your circle of yarn?"

"Using the floor to help you, can you make a pyramid with a square base?"

"Using the floor to help you, can you make a cube?"

"Two groups get together. One group makes a square with their yarn, the other group makes a triangle INSIDE of the square." (This is an effective way for students to compare/contrast various geometrical shapes and areas.)

LANGUAGE ARTS AND SOCIAL STUDIES

Teacher: *"We are going to use our circles of yarn to improve our writing ability by forming descriptors or adjectives. Using your circle of yarn and the people in your group, place the yarn on the floor. Let go of the yarn. Using the yarn, draw a simple outline of a butterfly."* (Students take a few moments to compare/contrast each completed butterfly on the floor.)

"Transform your butterfly into a SAD butterfly."

"Transform your SAD butterfly into a POWERFUL butterfly."

"Transform your POWERFUL butterfly into an INSIGNIFICANT butterfly."
(Teacher continues to announce various descriptors that fit the student's grade
level. Give students a few moments to compare/contrast each group's interpretation of the words.)

*"Now we are going to use our circles of yarn to improve our SPELLING. The first
word on our spelling list is HAPPY. Using your circle of yarn and the people in your
group, make a happy shape. Our next spelling word is the word ANGULAR. Can
you make an angular shape?"* (Teacher continues to announce spelling words that
each group can form into an appropriate shape. Words should be appropriate for
age and grade level of students.)

*"Now we are going to use our circles of yarn to improve our MAP skills. Lay your
circle of yarn on the floor. Let go of it. Using your circle of yarn and the people in
your group, draw an outline of the state of Illinois."* (Students take a few moments
to compare/contrast each completed map on the floor.)

"Can someone in your group point to the state capital, Springfield?"

"Can someone in your group trace the Mississippi River?"

*"Can someone in your group lay their hand on the county with the lowest
population?"*

*"Is someone in your group standing or sitting in Indiana? Is someone in Iowa?
Wisconsin? Kentucky?"*

"Two groups get together. Can one group make Indiana next to Illinois?"

*"Two groups get together. I will give one group a larger circle of yarn. Using the
larger circle of yarn, can one group make an outline of the state of Texas around the
map of Illinois? Now I will give one group a very small circle of yarn. Can one group
make the outline of the state of Connecticut inside of Illinois?"* (This is a very
effective way for students to compare/contrast the shapes of the various states.)

A fringe benefit of the Circle of Yarn activity is improved cooperative learning
and understanding of group dynamics.

"Seeing" Questions

Questioning can easily become a visual activity by using a teaching technique called webbing or mindMapping. MindMapping begins with simple brainstorming techniques. It presents a visual framework for those ideas from which a product is produced. The MindMap allows fantasy and imagination, language rhythms, patterns, associations, and metaphors to emerge into an organizational framework.

Sometimes in the brainstorming process, while questions and responses are being placed on the mindMap, the student has an *"aha"* experience, and a topic or central idea emerges.

Students who are visual learners will appreciate *"seeing"* their questions and responses on a graphic organizer.

Good Resources
IT'S ABOUT WRITING
© 1990
THEMATIC ACTIVITIES FOR
STUDENT PORTFOLIOS
© 1994
by Kathy Balsamo
Pieces of Learning

Government Question Web

Brainstorm all the ways to interest Congress in a law you want passed.

If you were a Senator how would you vote for...

Would you rather visit a Vietnam Memorial or a Civil War Memorial?

Compare and contrast Senate members with the Cabinet.

Imagine

Suppose

Substitute the present foreign policy toward Japan **for** a better one.

List the advantages of having less Congressmen. **(Minify)**

What if the Chairman of the Joint Chiefs of Staff had more power than the President? **(Reverse)**

?

How come...

Find out how automobiles run. What if the Postal Service was run the same way? **(Adapt)**

Combine ...and...

Rearrange the rooms of the White House and tell why you changed them.

Pretend you are the gavel of the Speaker of the House. Describe your most memorable day. **(How would this look, feel to ...)**

Enlarge...

Who... what...when... where... why

What can we use closed military bases for? **(Another Use)**

What would happen if there were only one Senator from each state?

How is the Supreme Court **like** the cherry trees in Washington D.C.?

From a Good Resource
THEMATIC ACTIVITIES FOR STUDENT PORTFOLIOS
© 1994
by Kathy Balsamo
Pieces of Learning

Government

Make a dictionary of government words that are important for a student to know. Make 7 ten-word sentences. Use one dictionary word in each sentence.

The Executive Branch has 12 departments. Make a calendar. For each month illustrate jobs in a branch.

Make a list of questions you would ask someone interviewing for a job in your prinicpal's office.

Survey student's parents. Tabulate results and graph the jobs parents have in local government.

Make a poster showing the 3 main branches of government and list 6 different jobs for each one.

Do a report on the history of the White House.

What is the National Endowment for the Arts? Does your city or school benefit from it? How? Would you like to? How could you help?

$ If you were in charge of the school budget how much money would you give to the principal, teachers, sports teams, science classes, and gifted classes? Give reasons to support your decisions.

Make a cartoon strip about what you would do if you were president.

Draw a map of Washington D.C. and label some important buildings. Make a model of one of the monuments.

Make fact cards about the government. Create a game from the cards.

What science research does the government pay for? Give an example of some research that affects you.

State a law you would like passed in your town. What steps do you have to take to get it passed? Do them! Keep a journal of the process.

Design a travel brochure describing all the important places to visit in Washington D.C.

From a Good Resource
THEMATIC ACTIVITIES FOR STUDENT PORTFOLIOS
© 1994
by Kathy Balsamo
Pieces of Learning

The Answer Is: FALL

Compose MANY DIFFERENT questions about FALL using the following VOCABU-LARY words. Be creative! Combine words from different categories. Add more words and categories if you want. Your questions should include **What if...?, Compare/Contrast statements, What are all the ways...?, How come...?, and Point of View**. Remember! The key words in active questioning are MANY and DIFFERENT.

Category:Holidays

Columbus	explorer
ocean	voyage
ship	crew
unknown	brave
Halloween	scared
skeleton	black cat
attic	cellar
ghost	pumpkin
Thanksgiving	feast
thankful	tradition
Pilgrims	elections
campaign	candidate
office	witches

Category: Weather

chill	frost
brisk	gust
rainy	dark
autumn	

Category: Animals

hibernate	migrate
south	hunting

FALL

Category: Sports

football	touchdown
team	cross country
soccer	field
stadium	win
lose	tennis

Category: Harvest

cider	haystack
apples	festivals
corn	wheat
orchard	ripe
Indian Corn	pumpkins

1._____

2._____

3. What if_____

4._____

5. How come_____

6._____

7. What are all the ways_____

8._____

9. I feel_____

10. How is_____like_____

The Answer Is: _____

Category:_____

_____

_____

_____

_____

Category:_____

_____

_____

_____

Category:_____

_____

_____

_____

Category:_____

_____

_____

_____

_____

Category:_____

_____

_____

_____

1._____

2._____

3. What if_____

 4._____

5. How come_____

6._____

7. What are all the ways_____

8._____

9. I feel_____

10. How is_____like_____

"SKINNY" Questions and "FAT" Questions

The purpose of active questioning is to increase the number of questions that children ask (fluency) plus raise the level of complexity and creativity (flexibility). Sometimes a complex process like questioning is made easier by simplifying the terminology. Students will have fun identifying basic recall, convergent, right answer questions as "Skinny" questions and more complex, divergent, open-ended questions as "Fat" questions. Appropriate illustrations along with different computer printing fonts will also help in the identification process.

WARNING:Teachers/parents, be sensitive to the needs of children who are overweight or underweight. As an overweight child myself, I have many painful memories of the cruelty of fellow classmates concerning my weight. The illustrations for "skinny" and "fat" questions should NEVER be of humans. Have a private talk with those students with obvious weight differences BEFORE using these lessons. If you feel there will be even a hint of a problem, by all means change the words skinny/fat to lean/plump, closed/open, narrow/wide, convergent/divergent, empty/full, weak/strong, type A/type B or low level/high level.

A Symbol for "Skinny" Questions

A Symbol for "Fat" Questions

SKINNY QUESTIONS

WHAT IS TWO PLUS TWO?

CAN YOU NAME THE ANIMAL CALLED MAN'S BEST FRIEND?

LIST THE CHARACTERS IN THE STORY GOLDILOCKS AND THE THREE BEARS.

WHAT COLOR IS MICKEY MOUSE'S NOSE?

WHAT ANIMAL LOOKS LIKE A HORSE BUT HAS STRIPES?

FAT QUESTIONS

What are all the ways you can think of to say four?

How are dogs and cats alike and different?

How would you feel if you found a bear hiding in your room?

What if your nose were on top of your head?

How come zebras have stripes but horses don't?

Be A Question Detective!

"Fat" questions have "fat" words in them. Some of the "fat" words to look for are:

rather	How come...
how many ways...	opinion
what if	reasons
feel	alike and different
feelings	What do you think?
compare	contrast
imagine	How do you feel?

Read the following "fat" questions. Circle all the "fat" words.

1. What if the game of baseball had no bases?
2. Would you rather play in a band or an orchestra? Why?
3. How do you feel when you see an animal that has been hurt?
4. How many ways can you eat ice cream?
5. Can you list many reasons why people watch TV?
6. How are worms and spaghetti alike and different?
7. How come cars can't fly?
8. Can you compare/contrast a drop of rain and the Pacific Ocean?
9. What do you think about when you see someone smoking?
10. How are you and your grandparents alike?

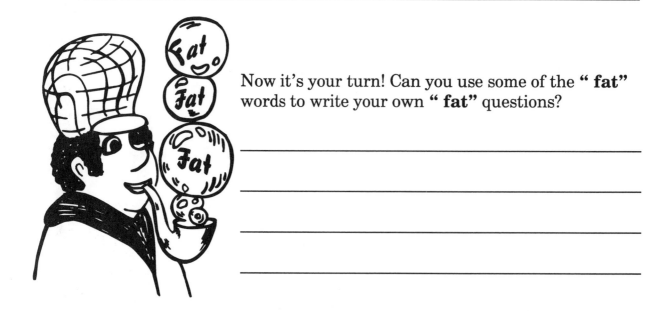

Now it's your turn! Can you use some of the " fat" words to write your own " fat" questions?

_____

_____

_____

_____

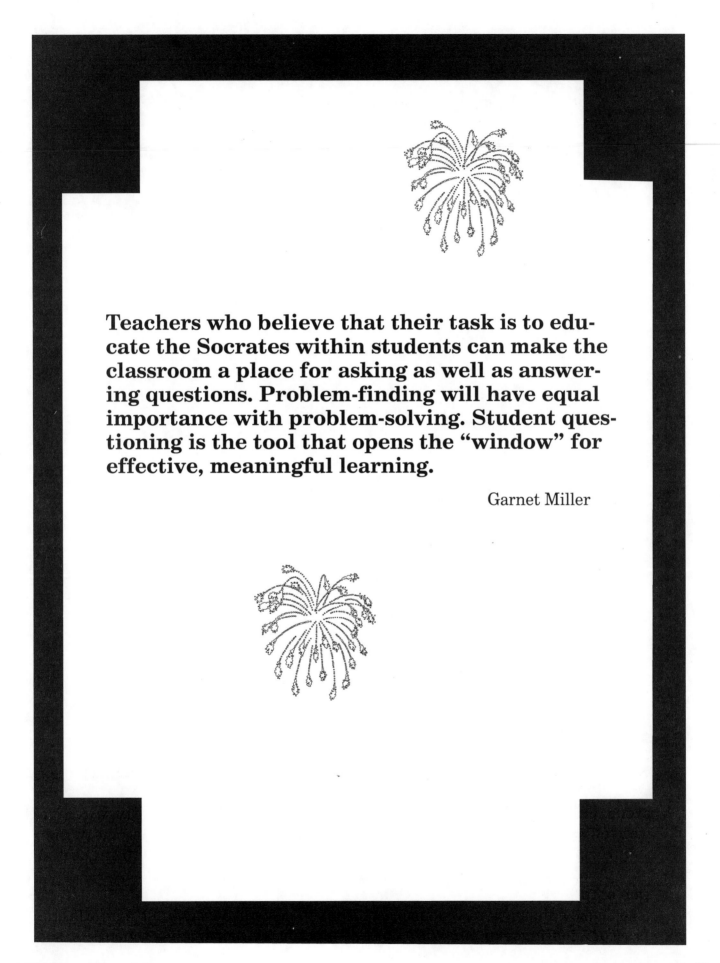

Teachers who believe that their task is to educate the Socrates within students can make the classroom a place for asking as well as answering questions. Problem-finding will have equal importance with problem-solving. Student questioning is the tool that opens the "window" for effective, meaningful learning.

Garnet Miller

Ask Me About Clouds

Read the questions.

Where are clouds?
How are clouds and cotton alike and different?
What is wet and drops from clouds in a storm?
How do storm clouds make you feel?
What if clouds could giggle?
What color are most clouds?

Copy each of the questions in the correct place.

SKINNY CLOUD QUESTIONS

1. Where are clouds?

2._____

3._____

FAT CLOUD QUESTIONS

1. How are clouds and cotton alike and different?

2._____

3._____

Now it is your turn! Make up your own "Skinny" and "Fat" questions.

_____

_____

Copy one fat cloud question and write or draw your response.

_____

_____

_____

Ask Me About Dinosaurs

Read the questions.

Are dinosaurs alive?
Are there books about dinosaurs in the library?
How would you feel if a dinosaur showed up in your back yard?
Can you name a dinosaur that was a meat eater?
What if dinosaurs could talk?
How are dinosaurs like a truck?
How are they different from a truck?

Copy the questions in the correct place.

SKINNY DINOSAUR QUESTIONS

1. Are dinosaurs alive?

2._____

3._____

FAT DINOSAUR QUESTIONS

1. How would you feel if a dinosaur showed up in your back yard?

2._____

3._____

Copy one fat dinosaur question and write or draw your response.

_____

_____

_____

Now it's your turn! Make up your own "Skinny" and "Fat" questions about dinosaurs.

_____

_____

Can you answer any of the dinosaur questions on this page?

Ask Me About _____?

(topic)

Read the questions.

_____

_____

_____

Copy the questions in the correct place.

Skinny _____ Questions

1. _____

2. _____

3. _____

Fat _____ Questions

1. _____

2. _____

3. _____

Copy one fat _____ question and write or draw your response.

_____

_____

_____

Now it's your turn! Make up your own "Skinny" and "Fat" questions about

_____.

_____

_____

Can you answer any of the _____ questions on this page?

Questioning Around the World
MEXICO

To the teacher: A thematic unit on the country of Mexico might begin with a class discussion or homework assignment requiring students to compose as many different questions as they can about Mexico. The lists of questions can serve as a pre-assessment for the unit; the number and type of questions will be a strong indicator of each student's knowledge base of Mexico. The lists can also be used as a student portfolio item.

The Question Piñata

Buy or construct a piñata. Cut a hole in the top of the piñata and fill it with questions. The following divergent, open ended, "fat" questions about Mexico can easily be cut apart in strips and used for the Question Piñata.

Compare and contrast the Rio Grande River and the Mississippi River.

Pretend you are your own stomach. Mexican food is on its way! How do you feel?

What if all peppers were not hot?

What if Mexico bordered Alaska?

Compare and contrast the Mexican hat dance with a country/western line dance.

How would you feel if part of your family lived in Mexico but you still lived here?

Compare and contrast Mexican chili with Texas chili and Cincinnati chili.

You are a desk in the office of the President of Mexico. What do you see and hear? What is your fondest memory?

What would happen if you received a piñata full of gold for your birthday?

What inventions would be useless to humans trying to survive in a Mexican or United States desert?

Compare and contrast the Navajo and Aztec cultures.

Congratulations! You just won a free trip to Mexico. Where would you go? Why?

What if all the gold in the world was in Mexico?

Compare/contrast the National Palace in Mexico City with the White House in Washington D.C.

What would you think if the United States and Mexico combined to form one country?

Why isn't there a wall like The Great Wall of China around the United States?

United States residents visiting Mexico may bring back articles for personal use valued at up to $400.00 free of duty. What would you shop for in Mexico if you were to visit? Suppose you could give $400.00 worth of gifts that best represented the United States to a Mexican student. List your choices.

List all the ways a student from the United States might find a pen pal in Mexico.

What are all the ways Mexico and the United States could be better friends?

What is NAFTA and what are your state's senators' opinions of it? Compose a survey about NAFTA and distribute it among family and friends.

The year is 1836. You are a gun in the Alamo. What kind of gun are you? Who is your owner? What do you see? How do you feel?

What would happen if the next Disney World was built in Mexico?

How is American football like Mexican football? How are they different?
What if all people in the United States could speak Spanish and all people in Mexico could speak English?

What if an ancient but authentic map were found and the border between the United States and Mexico was actually 300 miles north of the Rio Grande River?

Pretend you are a sombrero on "Pancho" Villa's head. What is your future?

Compare/contrast a sombrero, a United States western cowboy's hat, and a coonskin cap.

What if cacti had feelings?

In your opinion are United States citizens and Mexican citizens both Americans?

Active Questioning About MEXICO

Compose two questions:

...un director para el gobierno de Washington, D.C., le preguntaría a un director para el gobierno de la Ciudad de México.

_____

_____

...una tortilla de la Ciudad Juarez, Chihauhua, le preguntaría una tajada de pan de Knoxville, Tenn., o Dayton, Ohio.

_____

_____

..un locutor mexicano le preguntaría a un locutor de los Estados Unidos.

_____

_____

...un caballo de pura sangre de Kentucky le preguntaría un burro de Tijuana.

_____

_____

..una mujer de negocios de Richmond, Virginia, le preguntaría a una mujer de negocios de Acapulco, Guerrero.

_____

_____

...un poncho de la Ciudad Victoria, Tamaulipas, le preguntaría un impermeable de Houston, Tx

_____

_____

...un cartero de Grand Rapids, Michigan, le preguntaría a un cartero de Durango, Durango.

...un pez del Golfo de Campeche, Tabasco, le preguntaría un pez de Narragansett Bay, Rhode Island.

...un par de botas para nieve de Walker, Minnesota, le preguntaría un par de sandalias de Hermosillo, Sonora.

Componga una lista de preguntas para debatir que son apropiadas para un debate entre un estudiante norte americano en una escuela secondaria y un estudiante mexicano un una escuela secondaria.

Componga una lista de preguntas que le preguntaría antes de que se convertiría en un ciudadano mexicano. Componga una lista de preguntas que un ciudadano mexicano le preguntaría antes de que se convertiría en un ciudadano de los Estados Unidos.

Tickle Your Questioning Funny Bone

A Student Questioning Notebook or Journal

"Seriosity" is the enemy of creative thinking. The use of humor is a powerful tool for unlocking the creative questioning potential in students. The forms on page 73 when copied several times, cut and stapled, form a questioning notebook or journal. Students can draw their own creative covers. On each page of the notebook there is a stimulating divergent question provided by the teacher as well as space for a response. In order to make the questioning ACTIVE, there is also a space for students to compose their own questions. Sample questions are listed below.

What are all the ways we humans are funny?

How do you feel when you laugh?

Compare/contrast a laugh and a giggle.

What if laughter was against the law?

Would you rather have a national Tongue-Twister Day or Knock-Knock Joke Day? Why? Interview your friends and make a collection of Tongue-Twisters and Knock-Knock Jokes.

You are a big red nose on a clown's face. What do you see? What do you smell? How do you feel?

What are all the ways adults are funnier than kids?

Can you list five things that kids think are funny but adults do not?

You have just invented a giggle machine. What would you do with it?

What does the word sit-com mean?

Which television program do you think is the funniest? Why?

What if whipped cream came out of the shower instead of water?

How can animals and humans be funny in the same way?

What are all the things that a class clown does in school?

Would you rather be the best athlete in your class or be the class clown?

Can you make a list of words that are fun to say?

What if humans could only walk backwards?

Are Funny Cars in the racing industry really funny?

Would watching a four foot basketball player compete with seven foot players be funny? What if you were the four foot player?

Would you rather be Whoopi Goldberg or Garfield the cat? Why?

You are a famous stand-up comedian. What kind of jokes would you tell? What kind of jokes wouldn't you tell?

Would you rather see something funny or hear something funny? Why?

What is a practical joke? List examples. Have you ever played a practical joke on someone else? Have you ever been the victim of a practical joke?

Collect cartoons and others pictures that you think are funny. Show them to your friends. How many of them agreed with you?

Is it better to laugh at someone or be the one laughed at? Does laughter ever hurt?

Can you list ten words that describe how you feel when you are tickled?

What if you were a famous clown in the circus? What if you were Ronald McDonald? Is it easier to be funny if nobody knows it's really you?

Have you ever laughed till you cried?

How come some people are funnier than others?

Is humor ever silent?
Do you ever dream funny things?

Has something ever happened to you that was scary at first but then turned out to be funny?

What does the word slapstick mean?

What if humans were not ticklish?

What's the funniest Halloween costume you ever wore?

Think about advertising and commercials on radio and TV. What does the statement "Humor Sells" mean?

Which color in the rainbow do you think is funny?

Do you like to write funny stuff like limericks or riddles?

What if humans really did have a funny bone to tickle?

What is the funniest thing you ever saw? ...ever did? ...ever wanted to do?

Did you ever hit your Crazy Bone? Did it make you laugh?

A Question To Tickle Your Funny Bone For _____
(date)

_____
(question provided by teacher)

Student Response: _____

_____

_____

More Funny Bone Questions By _____
(student)

_____

_____

A Question To Tickle Your Funny Bone For _____
(date)

_____
(question provided by teacher)

Student Response: _____

_____

_____

More Funny Bone Questions By _____
(student)

_____

_____

Before and After Questions

Open-ended questions combined with graphic organizers are a fun way for students to sharpen their logical thinking skills. The concept of before and after questions can also be adapted to accommodate different uses and formats such as student journals, story starters and portfolio assessment. As always, be sure to take the activity to the **active** level by providing blank graphic organizers for students to use in creating their own before and after questions.

What comes before_____

_____

_____?

What comes after_____

_____

_____?

What comes before_____

_____

_____?

What comes after_____

_____

_____?

List of Questions

What comes after a funny joke?
What comes before you dial 911?
What comes after the telephone rings?
What comes before you say, "I'm sorry?"
What comes before the touchdown?
What comes after the electricity goes off?
What comes before the victory parade?
What comes after you are arrested?
What comes before payday?
What comes after the explosion?
What comes before the marathon race?
What comes before you sign the contract?
What comes after you hear, "Look out!"?
What comes before a broken arm?
What comes after drinking too much alcohol?
What comes before the homecoming parade?
What comes before opening night?
What comes after the summons?
What comes before the pizza is baked?
What comes after the fire alarm goes off?
What comes before you buy a car?
What comes after you join the Army?
What comes before the cure for a disease?
What comes after you lose your car keys?
What comes before a book becomes a best seller?
What comes after the invitations are sent?
What comes before the trophy is presented?
What comes after a tornado?
What comes before the concert?
What comes after the gunshot?
What comes before lift off?
What comes after the broken window?
What comes before the Halloween party?
What comes after the blender stops?
What comes before the Nobel Prize?
What comes after a squeaking door?
What comes before the opening curtain on stage?
What comes after a rainstorm?
What comes before the crowd gets angry?
What comes after the conductor raises her baton?
What comes after the apples are picked?
What comes before the ink pen runs dry?
What comes after the bowling ball hits the alley?
What comes before your grandmother comes for a visit?
What comes after you oversleep?

Before and After

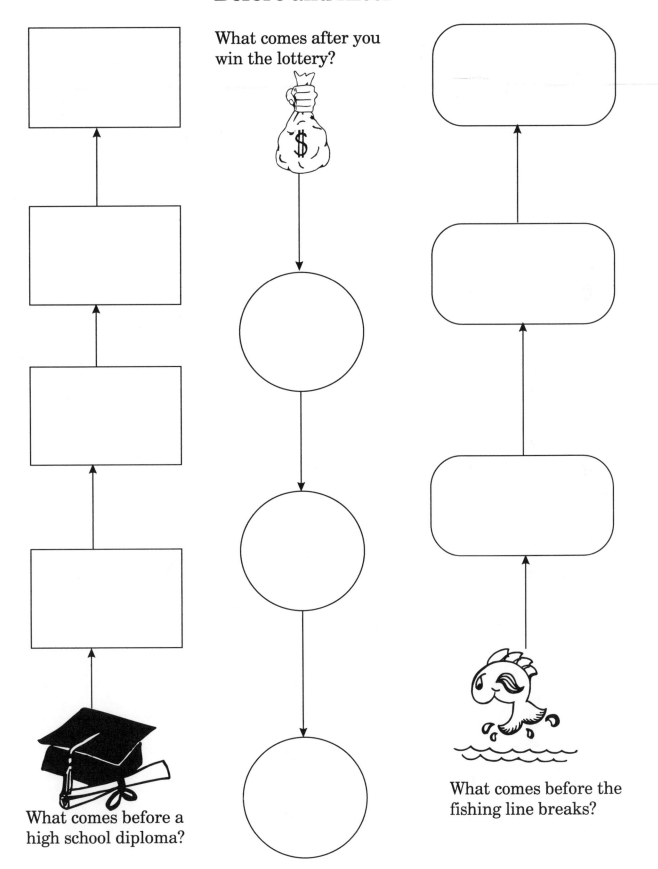

What comes after you win the lottery?

What comes before a high school diploma?

What comes before the fishing line breaks?

Before and After

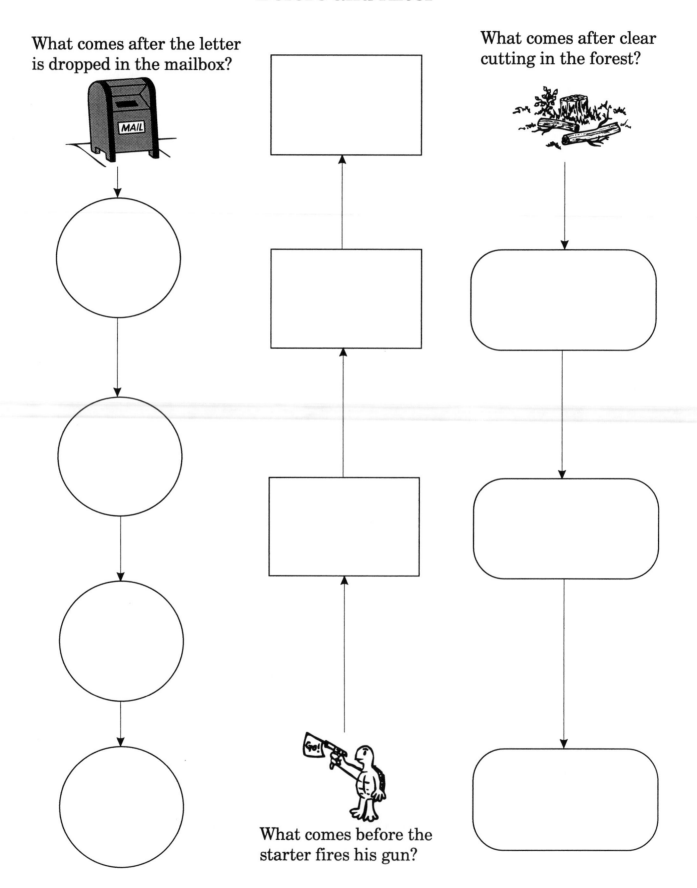

What comes after the letter is dropped in the mailbox?

What comes after clear cutting in the forest?

What comes before the starter fires his gun?

Before and After

What comes after_____

_____?

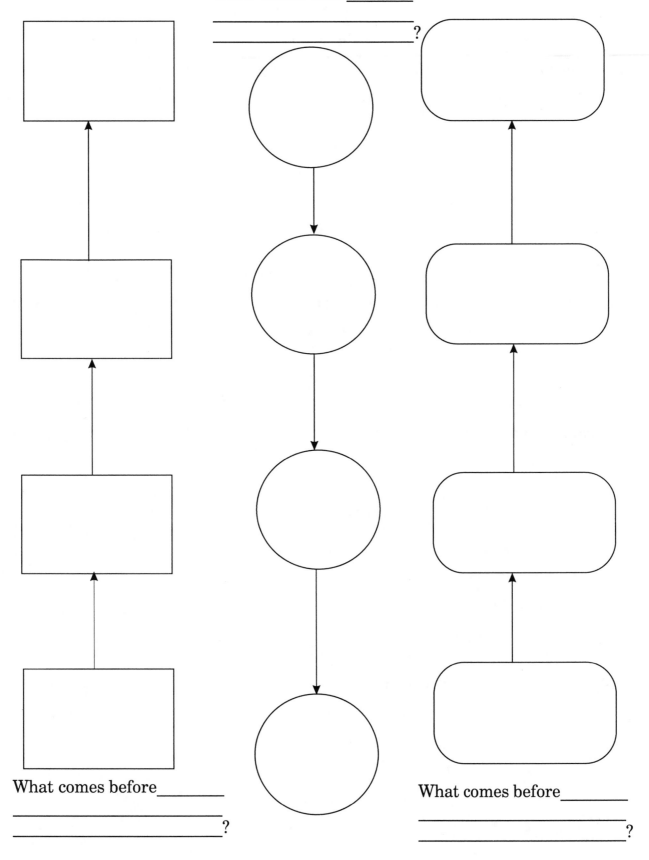

What comes before_____

_____?

What comes before_____

_____?

Questions About Jobs & Careers

Would you rather be a city commissioner, a health commissioner, or the commissioner of baseball? Why?

Would you rather be a congresswoman/congressman, a mayor, or a judge? Why?

Would you rather be a T.V. newscaster, a radio talk show hostess/host, or a movie director? Why?

Would you rather design video games, market and sell video games, or collect and repair old video games? Why?

Do you think some jobs or careers are just too dangerous for humans? Which ones? Make a list.

Do you agree or disagree with salary caps for professional athletes?

Would you rather be interviewed for a job or be the person doing the interviewing?

What if both of your parents lost their jobs? How would you feel? What would you do? How could you help? What would not be helpful?

Compare/contrast a manicurist with a farrier.

Would you rather have a good job in a foreign country or be unemployed in the United States?

What if you had to change careers three times in your life? Which careers would you choose? Which would you not choose?

Compare and contrast the duties of a swimming coach, a tennis coach, and a soccer coach.

Would you rather be a police detective, a private detective, or a writer of detective novels?

Would you rather have a job that paid big money but you really hated or a job that paid very little but you really loved?

What if you wanted a raise in your job? When, where, and how would you ask?

What do you think your first job and last job in your life will be?

Compare and contrast the salaries of males and females. Do you think it is all right for men to be paid more money than women when they do the same job?

What career would you like to have for only one week?

Would you rather be a cook in a Chinese, Italian, Indian, Mexican, or Greek restaurant?

Would you rather take a vocational class in electronics, health care, food service, auto mechanics, or child care?

Would you rather be an electrical engineer, a mechanical engineer, or a railroad engineer?

What if you were a research scientist? What would you like to research? Why?

Compare and contrast a make-up artist's tool box with a carpenter's tool box.

What job or career would you do for free? Why?

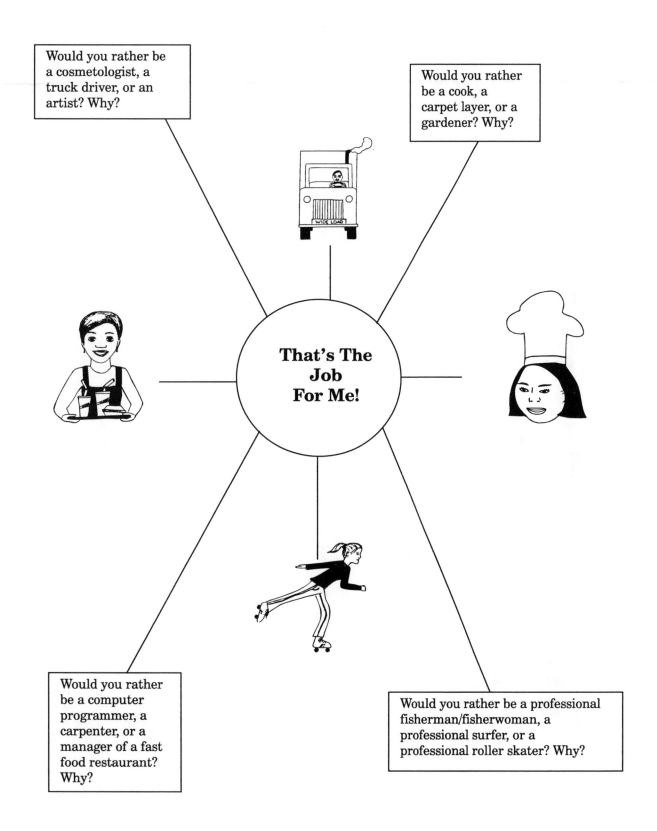

Would you rather be a cosmetologist, a truck driver, or an artist? Why?

Would you rather be a cook, a carpet layer, or a gardener? Why?

That's The Job For Me!

Would you rather be a computer programmer, a carpenter, or a manager of a fast food restaurant? Why?

Would you rather be a professional fisherman/fisherwoman, a professional surfer, or a professional roller skater? Why?

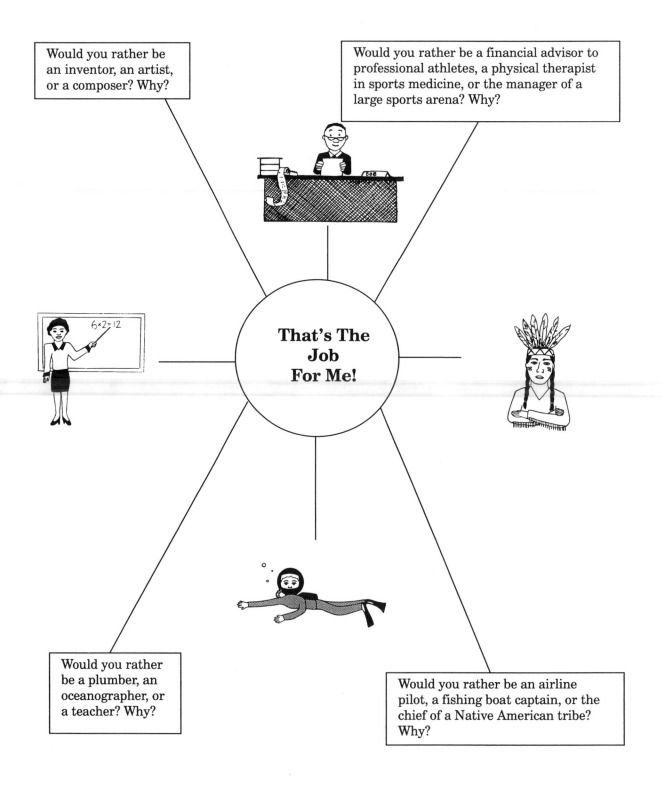

Would you rather be an inventor, an artist, or a composer? Why?

Would you rather be a financial advisor to professional athletes, a physical therapist in sports medicine, or the manager of a large sports arena? Why?

That's The Job For Me!

Would you rather be a plumber, an oceanographer, or a teacher? Why?

Would you rather be an airline pilot, a fishing boat captain, or the chief of a Native American tribe? Why?

Career Questioning

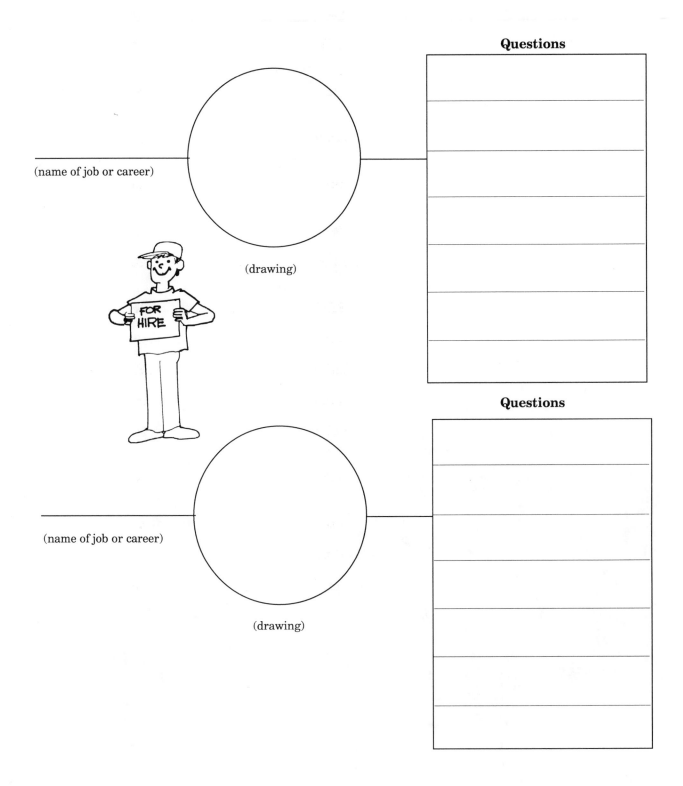

Questions

_____
(name of job or career)

(drawing)

Questions

_____
(name of job or career)

(drawing)

Picture! Picture!

Pictures or illustrations can be effective tools in stimulating active questioning. Look carefully at the picture below. Think about what you see. Think about what you don't see. Try to become part of the picture yourself. Don't hurry. Thinking and questioning takes time! When you are ready read each of the questions.

What is the girl on the left doing?
Is she just talking or telling a secret?
Are the kids in the picture friends?
Where are they going?
What might each child's name be?
What season of the year is it?
Who is the oldest?
Who is the youngest?
Are any of the kids brothers or sisters to each other?
How are the children's clothes alike and different?
How are the children's personalities alike and different?
Which kid is the coolest dresser?
What does the "U" stand for on the little boy's shirt?
Are all the kids happy?
How come there aren't any adults around?
What happened before the kids got together?
What are all the things that might happen after the girl finishes talking?
Will the oldest boy tell other kids what he is hearing?
Which child will most likely keep the secret?
When is it OK to tell a secret?
What would be a good title for this picture?

A Good Resource

IF YOU PROMISE NOT TO TELL
©1991
by Joe Wayman
Pieces of Learning

Picture! Picture!
What Questions Are You Hiding?

Look carefully at the picture below. Think about what you see.

Think about what you don't see. Try to become part of the picture yourself. Don't hurry! Thinking and questioning take time. When you are ready, write as **many different** questions as you can about the picture. Compare and contrast your questions with a classmate.

A Good Resource

Don't Burn Down The Birthday Cake
©1988
by Joe Wayman
Pieces of Learning

1. _____?

2. What   if_____?

3. _____?

4. How come_____?

5. _____?

6. What are all the ways_____?

7. _____?

8. I feel_____?

9. _____?

10. How is _____ like _____?

Picture! Picture!
What Questions Are You Hiding?

Look carefully at the picture below. Think about what you see.

Think about what you don't see. Try to become part of the picture yourself. Don't hurry! Thinking and questioning take time. When you are ready, write as **many different** questions as you can about the picture. Compare and contrast your questions with a classmate.

1._____?

2. What if_____?

3. _____?

4. How come_____?

5. _____?

6. What are all the ways_____?

7._____?

8. I feel_____?

9._____?

10. How is _____ like _____?

Don't Burn Down The Birthday Cake
by Joe Wayman

Picture! Picture!
What Questions Are You Hiding?

Look carefully at the picture below. Think about what you see.

Think about what you don't see. Try to become part of the picture yourself. Don't hurry! Thinking and questioning take time. When you are ready, write as **many different** questions as you can about the picture. Compare and contrast your questions with a classmate.

Don't Burn Down The Birthday Cake
by Joe Wayman

1._____?

2. What if_____?

3. _____?

4. How come_____?

5. _____?

6. What are all the ways_____?

7._____?

8. I feel_____?

9._____?

10. How is _____ like _____?

"Dear Kid Question,"

Practice! Practice! Practice! It takes lots of practice to become a good questioner. Students will have fun taking turns being Kid Question for a week. The teacher/facilitator chooses a student on Monday to be Kid Question for the week. A topic or theme for the questioning is shared with the class. Students submit their questions to Kid Question on the forms provided.

After gathering questions from classmates during the week, Kid Question shares his/her favorites on Friday. They also share several of their own personal responses. If Kid Question is stumped by some of the questions they can ask classmates for suggested responses. The responding to the questions can be done individually, in cooperative groups, or as a whole class lesson. The entire process takes on a "Dear Abby" flavor.

The teacher/facilitator can save the questions and topics from each week to be placed in a Dear Kid Question Catalog, Scrapbook, Diary, or class newspaper. If all goes well, by the end of the school year students will have a lot of creative questions to review. The thinking level can be raised even higher if the teacher/facilitator helps students categorize their questions. For example, questions could be categorized by type of question (What if...?, Point of View, Quantity, Compare/Contrast, or How come...?) humorous/serious, most unusual, craziest, most practical, most useful, longest, or most unique.

The topics or themes used to stimulate questioning should range from humorous and silly to puzzling and serious. Sometimes the craziest topic reaps the most questions. Obviously, different topics will appeal to different sexes, learning styles, ages, and grade levels. The teacher/facilitator should challenge the class to increase the number of questions they submit each week. The name of the game in ACTIVE QUESTIONING is QUANTITY or FLUENCY! The following list of topic and themes will get you started. Don't forget to allow students to suggest topics!

Topics and Themes
For "Dear Kid Question" Project:

Slime	Endangered Species	Bugs
Outer Space	Kid's Rights	Soccer
Steven Spielberg	Popcorn	Money
Sisters/Brothers	Spaghetti	Snow
Bubble Gum	Volcanos	TV
Sports	Mud	Floods

QUESTIONS!   QUESTIONS!   QUESTIONS!

Topic:_____Week Of:_____

Kid Question's Name:_____

Dear Kid Question,

_____

_____

_____

_____

_____

_____

_____

_____

_____

_____

_____

Sincerely,

?   _____

"How Come...?"

A Questioning Rainbow

How come rain falls in drops?
How come cats have nine lives?
How come spaghetti gets soft in hot water?
How come magnets attract?
How come neon signs glow?
How come people love rainbows so much?
How come there are rainbows?
How come bats don't run into things when they fly at night?
How come there are black holes in outer space?
How come some people are color blind?
How come rainbows aren't just one color?
How come rainbows don't last a long time?
How come the earth never slows down?
How come stars twinkle?
How come boomerangs come back?
How come stars don't fall?

A Pot of Questions

About Rainbows: Rainbows really aren't objects like trees or animals or clouds. Each person who looks at a rainbow sees something a little different. Their eyes see the rainbow of colors in an arc across the sky which is really light bent and reflected by zillions and zillions of tiny raindrops. The drops of rain act like prisms, separating sunlight into different colors as the light passes through them. Because rainbows are tricks of light each person sees a different rainbow made from the light rays streaming in from behind them and the raindrops in front of them. That makes a rainbow unique in the eyes of the beholder. The rainbow you see is yours alone!

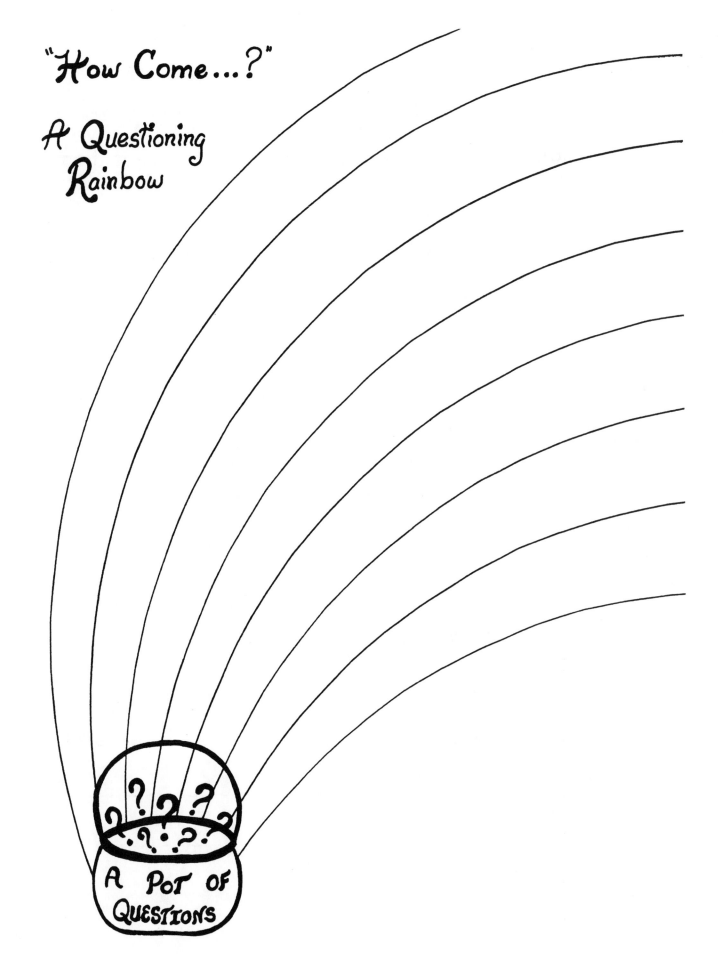

"How Come...?"

A Questioning Rainbow

A Pot of Questions

BEARS! BEARS! BEARS!

Look at this "BEARY" good picture about BEARS. Making up questions about BEARS is a "BEARY" good idea. You will have "BEARLY" enough space to write your "BEARY" good questions about BEARS! Just "BEAR" with it. The giggles you will feel will be unBEARable!

→

Why_____?

How come_____?

I wonder if_____?

Why can't_____?

When will the_____?

What if_____?

How is_____ like_____?

How is_____ different from_____?

Where did_____?

What are all the ways_____?

How in the world_____?

Who will_____?

Got any Questions?

_____

_____

_____

_____

_____

_____

_____

_____

It's A Questioning Puzzle
All About Math!

Read the questions on the puzzle pieces. Write your responses on a separate piece of paper. Just for fun, cut out the puzzle and put it together!

List all the words you can think of that are part of the study of mathematics.

Compare/contrast addition, subtraction, multiplication and division.

Pretend you are an inch worm. List all the things you <u>COULDN'T</u> measure.

You are a Super Hero. Your name is Action Fraction. Write three story problems about your adventures with fractions.

Collect several jigsaw puzzles. Calculate the average time it takes you and your friends to put together a 100, 500, and 1000 piece puzzle. Graph the results.

You have just been elected to the MATH HALL OF FAME. Why? Describe your math talent.

You are a math detective. How many uses of math in your life can you detect? List and explain.

The answer is **10**. How many DIFFERENT math problems can you create?

The Guinness Book of World Records asks you to create the worlds longest, most unusual word math problem. Try It!

Would you rather solve ONE hard math problem or 30 easy ones? Why?

A Question Puzzle by _____

(topic, theme or idea)

After completing the questions, write a report or story about your topic. Draw a picture on the back of the puzzle.

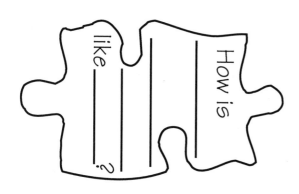

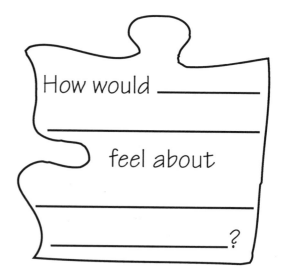

How come _____
_____
_____
_____?

How is _____
different from
_____
_____?

Why_____
_____
_____
_____?

I wonder_____
_____
_____
_____?

List as many
_____
_____
_____
_____

More Puzzle Questions

What's good about rainy days and Mondays?

How would growing up on a farm be different from growing up in the suburbs?

What if kids could pass laws? Propose a new law that kids your age would have to obey.

List all the ways you can think of to get what you want for your next birthday.

Do you think there is life on other planets? Explain your point of view.

What if you were in a department store and you saw someone shoplift?

Would you rather be an only child, the youngest child, or the oldest child in a family?

Compare and contrast living at the bottom of the sea with living in outer space.

What if you got the chicken pox every time you touched anything blue?

The Question Puzzle

To the student: _____

_____

_____

Questions By The Deck!

To the Teacher:

The sentences on the following deck of 52 cards are **Quantity, Compare/Contrast, What if...?, Point of View, and How come...?** questions. The six pages of cards can be duplicated, cut apart, and laminated creating a complete deck of cards for each student. Before the pages are laminated students personalize each card by printing another question on the back of each one or decorating the back with their own designs.

On the front of each card are two small boxes. Students draw a symbol for each suit inside the boxes. For example, instead of diamonds, hearts, clubs, and spades students may choose stars, clovers, jack-o-lanterns, and snowmen. Animals, leaves, people, names, letters or any creative symbol or shape will work.

The deck of cards can be used as flash cards or to play simple card games like "Go Fish," "Rummy" or "War". Students can also combine their deck of cards with a simple game board to create a new game.

1 — Make a list of holidays and festivals we don't celebrate but should.

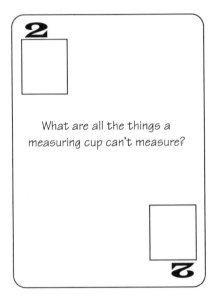

2 — What are all the things a measuring cup can't measure?

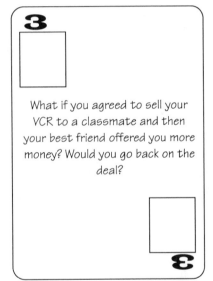

3 — What if you agreed to sell your VCR to a classmate and then your best friend offered you more money? Would you go back on the deal?

4 — List five things that would make school a better place to learn.

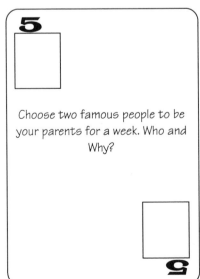

5 — Choose two famous people to be your parents for a week. Who and Why?

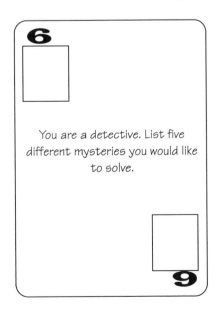

6 — You are a detective. List five different mysteries you would like to solve.

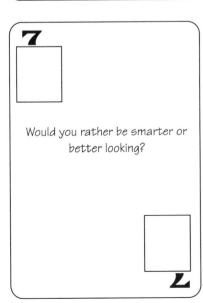

7 — Would you rather be smarter or better looking?

8

What if all automobile drivers in the United States had to drive on the left side of the road every Tuesday?

8

9

What questions would you be scared to ask somebody because of the answer you might get? Is there ever a time when trusting grown-ups is impossible?

9

10

When dealing with a conflict, which is easier: fighting, negotiating, or walking away? Which is smarter?

10

11

When does speed save lives? When does it take lives?

11

12

List 10 things you could do in the next two weeks that would guarantee an invitation to a party or school dance.

12

13

Under what circumstances would you "draw a line in the sand," stand your ground and fight to the death?

13

1

You are living 100 years in the future. List five questions to ask the people living in 1995.

1

2

Do you think girls or boys have it easier?

2

3

What if you were the leader of the largest, most powerful gang in your city?

3

4

Are you good at giving excuses? List your five best.

4

5

Do you think it is possible for children to be models for their parents? When? Why?

5

6

What if your parents were addicted to illegal drugs? What could you do? What should you do? What wouldn't you do?

6

7

List all the chores and jobs around the house that you DON'T have to do.

7

8

Do you own a lucky charm? Have you ever been the victim of bad luck?

8

9

List five questions a seatbelt might ask a pair of suspenders.

9

10

Would you rather be a world class athlete in an individual sport or a team sport?

10

11

List five memories you wish you had.

11

12

Compare and contrast dreams and nightmares.

12

13

What if someone else had to pick out the clothes you wore everyday to school? Who would you want that person to be?

13

1

List five times when you wish you had kept your mouth shut.

1

2

Do you like your age? What age is the best age to be?

2

3

What would happen if you were the school custodian for a week? What changes would you make?

3

4

What if you were a twin? List ways your life would be different.

4

5

What if you were the first student in space?

5

6

If you could only save ONE endangered animal, which animal would it be? Why?

6

7

Would you rather be really smart or a really hard worker?

7

8

List five reasons you would refuse to be friends with someone.

8

9

List five reasons why your parents should give you more allowance.

9

10

Who would YOU miss the most if you died? List five people who would miss you.

10

11

What does "we learn from our mistakes" mean?

11

12

Pretend you are a garbage collector in charge of collecting worthless ideas, notions, opinions, and feelings. Make a list of what you collected and where.

12

13

Compare/contrast winning and losing.

13

1

Do you think you are more like your father or your mother?

1

2

What are all the ways you can think of to change someone's mind.

2

3

Do you collect things? What collections would you like to have?

3

4

What if you could give your best friend a perfect day? Describe the day in writing and give it to your friend.

4

5

What if your mother painted her nails purple, wore green lipstick, and dyed her hair orange? Where would you go with her in public? Where wouldn't you go?

5

6

Design two billboards and four bumper stickers that reflect your point of view about life and the world.

6

7

List 5 ways to speed up school. List 5 ways to slow it down.

7

8

What if you promise your parents that you will wear a seatbelt when you ride in your friend's car, but when you get in the car none of the other riders are wearing theirs?

8

9

When is it really hard to ask questions?

9

10

Would you rather have your face appear on a fifty dollar bill or a postage stamp? Why?

10

11

Congratulations! You have just won five free ten minute phone calls to anyone, anywhere in the world. They must talk to you. Who would you call?

11

12

What if all humans had to migrate in the spring and fall?

12

13

List all the things you can do now that you couldn't do four years ago.

13

106

Questioning "Trading" Cards

To the Teacher:

The following set of 13 cards begins as a set of worksheets which students complete to practice their active questioning skills. The questions might fit a specific theme or topic. When duplicated four or more times and cut apart, they result in a set of questioning cards that students can trade or collect like baseball cards. Students enjoy personalizing their cards by adding a design on the back that incorporates their name, favorite TV character, sport, or food.

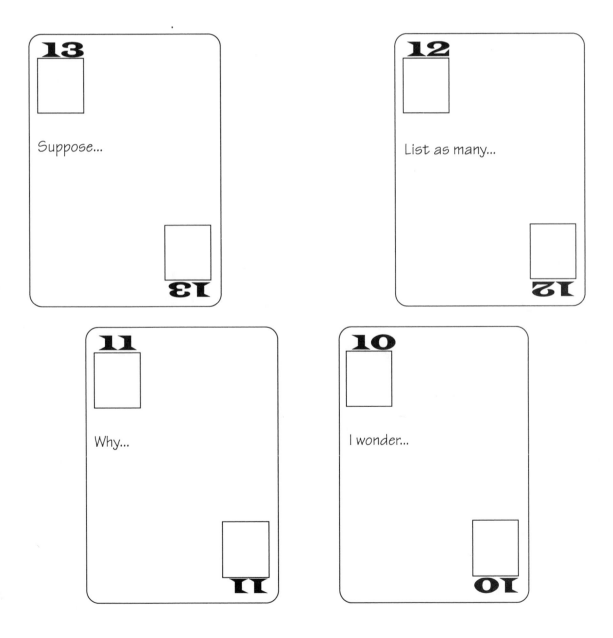

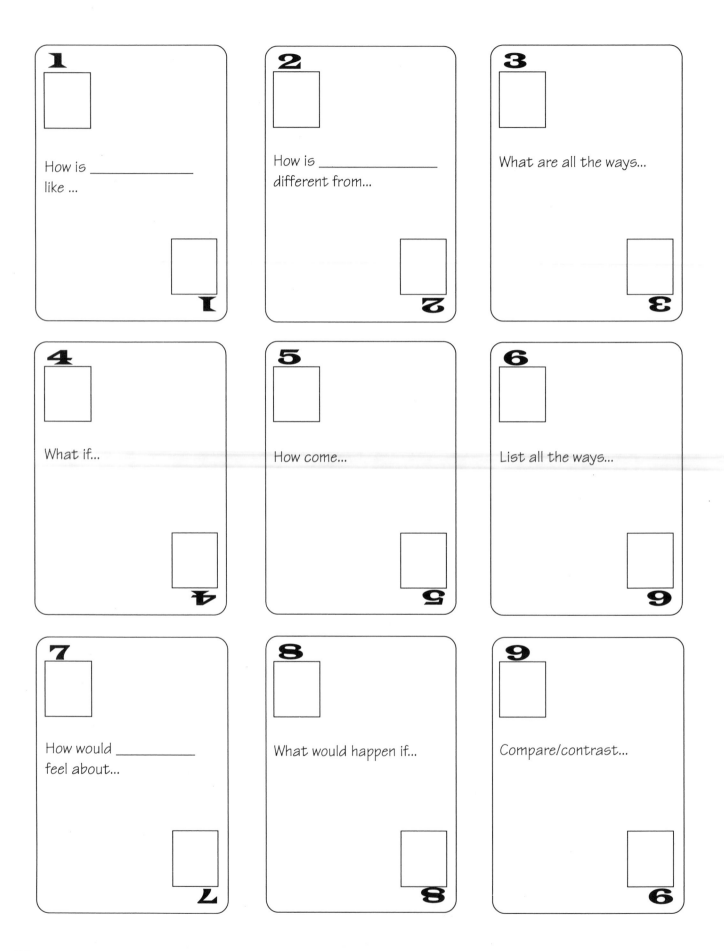

1

How is _____ like ...

2

How is _____ different from...

3

What are all the ways...

4

What if...

5

How come...

6

List all the ways...

7

How would _____ feel about...

8

What would happen if...

9

Compare/contrast...

108

More Questioning "Trading" Cards

To the Teacher:

The following set of 13 picture cards begins as a set of worksheets that students use to practice their active questioning skills. After duplicating the set of 13 cards and cutting them apart, students compose questions on the back of each card that relate to the picture on the front. Encourage students to compose and collect as many different kinds of questions as possible. Once again, the cards can be traded or collected like baseball cards. For example, if a student has several **What if...?** questions, he/she might try to trade for a **Point of View** question.

Teachers!

Be Strong!

Do not insist that students answer the questions they create.

Remember!

It's the skill of questioning that needs improvement, not the skill of answering.

REFERENCES

Balsamo, Kathy. THEMATIC UNITS FOR STUDENT PORTFOLIOS. Beavercreek, Ohio: Pieces of Learning, 1994.

Balsamo, Kathy. IT'S ABOUT WRITING. Beavercreek, Ohio: Pieces of Learning, 1990.

Christenbury, L. and Kelly, P. QUESTIONING, A PATH TO CRITICAL THINKING. Urbana, Illinois: ERIC, 1983.

Coil, Carolyn. PUT ON YOUR GLOBAL GLASSES: EYE ON JAPAN. Beavercreek, Ohio: Pieces of Learning, 1994.

Dillon, J.T. "The Effect of Questions In Education and Other Enterprises." JOURNAL OF CURRICULUM STUDIES, 1982. Pages 14, 127-152.

Dillon, J.T. "The Remedial Status of Student Questioning." JOURNAL OF CURRICULUM STUDIES, 1988. Pages 197-210.

Eberle, Bob. SCAMPER. East Aurora, New York: D.O.K, 1971.

Gall, Meredith. "Synthesis of Research on Teachers' Questioning." EDUCATIONAL LEADERSHIP, November, 1984. Page 43.

Johnson, Nancy. QUESTIONING MAKES THE DIFFERENCE. Beavercreek, Ohio: Pieces of Learning, 1990.

Johnson, Nancy. THINKING IS THE KEY. Beavercreek, Ohio: Pieces of Learning, 1992.

Johnson, Nancy. THE BEST TEACHER STUFF. Beavercreek, Ohio: Pieces of Learning, 1993.

Milios, Rita. IMAGI-SIZE. Beavercreek, Ohio: Pieces of Learning, 1993.

Miller, G.W. and Himsl, R. USER'S GUIDE FOR MEASURE OF QUESTIONING SKILLS. Joint Project for University of Georgia and Alberta Education, 1989.

Nash, W.R. and Torrance, E.P. "Creative Reading and The Questioning Abilities of Young Children." JOURNAL OF CREATIVE BEHAVIOR, 1974. Pages 15-19.

Stock, Gregory. THE BOOK OF QUESTIONS. New York, New York: Workman Publishing, 1987.

Wayman, Joe. DON'T BURN DOWN THE BIRTHDAY CAKE. Beavercreek, Ohio: Pieces of Learning, 1988.

Wayman, Joe. IF YOU PROMISE NOT TO TELL. Beavercreek, Ohio: Pieces of Learning, 1991.